SAY LESS, **GET MORE**

SAY LESS, GET MORE

Unconventional Negotiation Techniques
to Get What You Want

FOTINI ICONOMOPOULOS

Collins

Published by Collins, an imprint of HarperCollins Publishers Ltd

First published by Collins in a hardcover edition: 2021
This trade paperback edition: 2022

HarperCollins books may be purchased for educational, business, or sales
promotional use through our Special Markets Department.

HarperCollins Publishers Ltd
Bay Adelaide Centre, East Tower
22 Adelaide Street West, 41st Floor
Toronto, Ontario, Canada
M5H 4E3

www.harpercollins.ca

Library and Archives Canada Cataloguing in Publication

Title: Say less, get more : unconventional negotiation techniques to get what you want /
Fotini Iconomopoulos. | Names: Iconomopoulos, Fotini, author.
Description: Previously published: Toronto, Ontario, Canada: Collins, 2021.
Identifiers: Canadiana 20220203180 | ISBN 9781443464581 (softcover)
Subjects: LCSH: Negotiation in business.
Classification: LCC HD58.6 .I36 2021 | DDC 658.4/052—dc23

Printed and bound in the United States of America
LSC/H 9 8 7 6 5 4 3 2 1

To my family, who sealed my fate by giving me loads of negotiation practice and without whom this book would not be possible

CONTENTS

INTRODUCTION

NEGOTIATION IS EVERYWHERE

ON JANUARY 1, 2017, WHILE I WAS BACK HOME VISITING MY big fat Greek family and celebrating the annual New Year's Day feast at my cousin's house, I bolted for the door, EpiPen still in hand, after reacting to a pecan that was hiding in some unsuspecting dessert (curse you, sweet tooth!). I shouted, "I'm going to the hospital—allergic reaction!" My poor mother barely had time to run after me, yelling, "I'm coming with you!"

It wasn't the first time I'd landed myself in the emergency room, though it was the first time my mother had witnessed it. She may have lost a few years off of her life that day as she watched me drive across town at record speed. (Side note: If this career doesn't work out, I could become a race-car driver). Fortunately, before you could finish saying the words "anaphylactic reaction," I'd sailed past the broken limbs and chest pains and moved to the top of the triage list in the ER. (An EpiPen provides just one shot of adrenaline, and it's not always enough to stop an allergic reaction.)

There I was, supposedly the next person to be admitted, and yet I was waiting. Every second, my throat was scratchier, my nose was getting congested and my eyes were getting itchier (and my mom was starting to nervously rock in her chair). I could have just sat there until my name was called, as instructed by the receptionist, and waited for these reactions to get worse and my stress levels to increase, thus worsening the effects—not to mention the amount of recovery time I would need.

I'm not sure how many minutes had passed since I'd made first contact with the woman holding the key to my relief, but I sure as hell wasn't going to follow some rules that were allowing my throat to close and my eyes to start closing too. If you've ever seen the movie *Hitch* with Will Smith, I was well on my way to that punched-in-the-face-by-Rocky look. On top of that, I was now managing my worried mother's reaction to the whole situation: "When are they going to take you? What did she say? How much longer?" Nope. Not having it. Not that day.

At that moment I could have tried a number of approaches. Following the alpha-male "art of negotiation" model most often shown on TV and in movies, I could have banged my fist on the table and demanded better care, telling the receptionist, "I want to speak to your manager," or "If you don't get me in front of a doctor immediately, I'm going to sue everyone in here." Perhaps that would work for some people, particularly of the male, white-privileged variety. It could also prolong my wait.

Or I could have pushed my way through the trauma room doors and yelled, "I need a doctor, STAT!"—a real possibility with all the adrenaline already coursing through my veins from that first EpiPen. That approach might have gotten me removed by security and/or sedated before I got my next dose of epinephrine, a delay I didn't have the time for.

The good news is, I've had the benefit of studying and practicing negotiation under some pretty intense circumstances, so I was able to pause and consider the most beneficial course of action. With the few seconds it took me to think it through, I walked up to the receptionist and asked, "My throat is starting to get itchy again and it's been over twenty minutes since my first EpiPen; what can we do to get me back there faster?"

And with that, the curtain magically opened and I was ushered into . . . another waiting area. This time a triage nurse was waiting to do some more intake before I could make it to the promised land of doctors and IVs. In between my incessant sneezes, I managed to say, "I'm feeling wheezy. Can my mother answer any of these questions for you to speed this up?" And within minutes I was behind the curtain, getting my second shot of adrenaline.

Fortunately, after a third shot and five hours of observation, I managed to go home to my own bed for the night. Had I not expedited the steps of care I was to receive, my symptoms would have been more severe, requiring more recovery time, a night in the hospital with no sleep and another two days of sleep-inducing antihistamine doses. The longer it takes to get treatment, the worse my symptoms and recovery time.

On my drive home, I had an aha moment: Negotiation isn't always about cash. I had just negotiated my quality of life. Although I'm confident that I wouldn't have died if I'd had to wait longer in that emergency room, I wasn't willing to lose the next several days to sleeping off the medication. In addition to costing me time with family and friends, that extra recovery time and lost productivity could have affected my business for months to come. I knew what was at stake if I didn't find ways to work around the system, so sitting back and doing things someone else's way was not an option I was willing to accept.

Hospital emergency rooms are busy, often chaotic places. The person on the other side of the desk has to balance competing demands, so my task is to get an agreement on how my care should be prioritized within that mix. That is a negotiation that is far more valuable than anything I have ever been asked to do by my clients.

You see, negotiations aren't always about cash. And they happen all around us more often than you realize. In most of the negotiations we face every day, money never even exchanges hands, yet they can be life-changing. So many of the folks I encounter tell me that the thought of negotiating fills them with fear. That fear is understandable, but if you learn how to handle it, negotiating can help you reduce your stress and increase your quality of life.

Not everyone needs the experience of having to negotiate for their health in such a direct way, but there are plenty of times that you, dear reader, have had to negotiate to keep your sanity. If you've ever spent time around children (your own or others'), I guarantee you have negotiated for peace and quiet. I don't have kids of my own, but I have plenty of nieces and godchildren who have given me plenty of practice.

And boy, was I a handful for the adults in my life. I was nicknamed "the Negotiator" as a child, a title earned from my father. I can make a living by helping people get what they want because I was so practiced at doing it for myself and others. I had the strict upbringing of *My Big Fat Greek Wedding* (Nia Vardalos nailed my adolescence). If I wasn't speaking up for myself to get around all of the irrational rules, I was negotiating on behalf of my big sister and others around me. My father's first response whenever he realized what was happening was always, "I didn't ask for you to jump in, Negotiator."

I negotiated playdates, curfews, extracurricular activities, school trips, the ability to go away to university—it was all a careful game of chess that I played on a daily basis in our home. If your kids are driving you nuts, just remember that they may someday call the telecom company on your behalf to negotiate a cheaper phone bill.

YOU HAVE MORE PRACTICE THAN YOU REALIZE

Most of my clients, especially the women, tell me they don't have much experience negotiating, but that's just not true. We negotiate all the time, especially with children. I use a lot of child-related analogies when I'm preparing clients for high-stakes corporate negotiations—what works at home works in the boardroom, and vice versa. There have been times when family and friends have called me the "baby whisperer" because I practice what I preach. The negotiations at home are far more dramatic than the billion-dollar deals I have advised on. If you can handle a kid's temper tantrum, you can handle any negotiation with the adults at work.

Even without children in your life, there are plenty of everyday opportunities to negotiate your way to a less stressful life. What about wait times while you're getting your oil changed? Rescheduling your dinner reservation to leave enough time to pick up that birthday cake on the way to the restaurant so that you aren't the worst friend ever? Or maybe it's talking to the hotel clerk to get moved to the quiet floor so that the party bus of tourists who just checked in don't keep you up all night. These are all seemingly small-stakes negotiations that add up over time.

Ask yourself: What negotiations are you avoiding that are causing you to burn out? What are the little things you could be negotiating that could have an even more dramatic impact on your day-to-day life? Avoiding, or not even being aware of, these negotiation opportunities that surround us every day is the equivalent of death by a thousand cuts. Going after what you want, on the other hand, is your key to well-being.

If the thought of negotiating makes you anxious, you're not alone. Luckily, negotiation skills can be learned and practiced. This book will teach you the strategies and processes I've learned during the past few decades. Some of them I learned because I had to—because I found out early in my career that some of the tactics that I was being taught did not work for me as a woman with a funny name who looks visibly "different" from my older, white counterparts. This is an important distinction to make. Just as assertiveness is prized in white males but too often used to frame women as "bitchy," we must recognize that the same behavior and approaches from "different" people may/will often be received differently. This book will teach you concepts and processes that work for everyone. Each section will build on the previous one, so you'll want to read the chapters in order instead of bouncing around. Each section ends with a summary of main points that you can use as guideposts to keep you on track.

———

Imagine what life would be like if, armed with all of this knowledge and preparation, you could silence the fear that used to creep in at the thought of negotiating? That is what this book is about. It's about giving you the tools that will help you create moments of pause and clarity when you're about to freak out and start running for the hills. And it's about realizing that situations that will increase your personal well-being and wealth happen all around us. They're not limited to the dramatic boardroom scenes you might see in an episode of *Suits*. Negotiation opportunities abound every day and everywhere. And the knowledge offered in the chapters ahead represents your path to success.

SECTION 1

BREAKING DOWN THE BASICS

CHAPTER 1

FINDING THE ON-RAMP

I'VE BEEN NEGOTIATING MY ENTIRE LIFE—JUST ASK MY parents—but it wasn't until I was in my twenties that it finally clicked that I was surrounded by negotiation *all the time*. Often, we don't realize that we're in the middle of a negotiation until we stop to wonder what the hell just happened. The everyday situations we find ourselves in don't immediately fit our preconceived notions of negotiation. Another important insight, one that escapes many self-proclaimed experts, is that negotiating looks a little different depending on who is involved.

Whether I was working in consulting, manufacturing or retail, my colleagues were often tall, white, older men, and I was usually the youngest in the room, often by more than a decade. For a long time, I also happened to be the only one with a non-anglophone name, one that was so hard to pronounce, it wasn't unusual for me to be assigned an email address that was the only one in the company to follow the format firstname@company.com. I was like the Cher or Madonna of the company. Even in high school, if I got called over the PA system it was "Fotini . . . you know who you are . . . please report to the main office." I was different.

When I started consulting for and training high-level managers and executives, I would shadow my tall, male peers and mimic them word for word. I even dressed like them to ensure that the clients would have a consistent experience.

After a rigorous bootcamp of training, I was finally ready to run my own workshop. I was all alone, in a Marriott hotel in the Midwest, wearing the business-formal uniform—in my case a black suit with my hair tied back in a severe bun, in an attempt to look as polished and authoritative as I could, given that I was twenty to thirty years younger than my clients. I walked up to the seven men and one woman and said my first words: "Are you the negotiators?" To which everyone (who was, of course, there to attend a negotiation training) was expected to answer in the affirmative. When they did, I mimicked my peers with my next line, which was "We'll see."

You should know that every time I watched my tall, white, male peers say this, the unanimous response from the clients was . . . nothing. Perhaps a look of puzzlement or surprise, with an undertone of "This is going to be interesting," but that was it; people were put off just enough to be intrigued but not enough to rebel. On my first time out, I, the five-foot-five, ethnic-looking young woman, got a very different response. As the clients and I were walking down the hall to our meeting room, one gentleman shouted to his colleagues, "Did that fucking bitch just say, 'We'll see?'"

In that moment, I realized we were having our first negotiation of the week. My trainees would either follow me to the meeting room and compliantly continue with the program or begin a rebellion that would escalate after every instruction. I had no clue what to expect. I had never experienced this in my training. No one had prepared me for this kind of pushback. Every other tutor I'd watched had had the group following them like sheep. I thought someone was playing a trick on me, as a rookie hazing prank, but no one popped up from around the corner to say, "Got you!" That's when I knew it was on: the "fucking bitch" versus the [insert expletive] client.

I knew my next action would dictate how successful the rest of this week would be. My reaction could trigger a chain reaction, escalating the situation, or it could keep the training moving productively forward. My head was spinning with doubt and anger—which I knew was the name-caller's intention—but I managed to press my mental pause button to maintain my composure and carry on unrattled for the next three days.

I could have met fire with fire. I'm not one to shy away from a witty comeback, and I certainly don't hesitate to defend myself. But this situation felt different. As I played through the outcomes of various possible scenarios in my head (at record speed), I could see that none of them would end well. Reactive behavior breeds reactive behavior. It reminded me of when my big sister would try to annoy me to get under my skin. She'd hold her hand inches from my face and say, "I'm not touching you!" If I reacted, she'd laugh and then do it again—worse. If I maintained my composure, she'd grow tired and move on. When I paused to reflect on this experience, it made it easy to choose the most effective path. I refused to acknowledge what went down in any way because doing so would have given the name-caller just enough momentum to push further. So,

I was stoic—unflinching in my expression even though my mind was racing. As the session went on, I adjusted my language and navigated a few more challenging moments, the participants fell in line, and I carried on the workshop on my own terms—literally. I even ended up building such great relationships with the clients that they insisted on helping me pack up my things and taking me to the airport. In hindsight, they could have just been making sure I was getting the hell out of their country, but I'd like to remember it fondly as the situation that I managed to turn around with my behavior and charms. You decide.

Comfortably settled into the airport bar, I called a colleague to recount the story with all of the appropriate shock of being called those dreadful words. I told him I didn't think I would say "we'll see" again. That phrase wasn't being received in the same way when I delivered it as when my peers did. We wondered if the issue might be merely a flaw in my delivery, that I was being patronizing and condescending in some way. Duh. That cheeky line was intended to be exactly that. And my delivery in this situation was *exactly* the same as the ones I had observed before me.

What I knew in that moment, that others who hadn't been in my shoes had yet to grasp, was that the techniques used, the arrogance and haughtiness, did not work for everyone in every circumstance. Those words, which worked as intended when delivered by white, middle-aged males to a white male audience, did not play out the same way when you changed the players. When the presenter is a young Canadian woman of ethnic descent, and the audience is in Middle America, an area known to expect niceness, you've got a double whammy! The message was no longer received the way it was intended. It's something I'd known on a subconscious level for years. I had been surrounded by male negotiators and mentors throughout my childhood and career, but I was never so compelled to mimic their style, and when I finally did it backfired. In this instance, even in a professional corporate environment with a history of success, it blew up in my face.

I knew from then on that my approach needed to change, ever so subtly. I had to find my own voice and make modifications accordingly.

I never again said "we'll see" (in that context), even though I ran a lot of workshops during the next few years. My client evaluations only got better after I started to make tiny modifications to find my own voice, one that had a much more significant effect on those I was training. I started to pick up on all sorts of phrases and mannerisms that got different reactions than when men delivered them. It's important to note that, for many of us, emulating our negotiation role models doesn't always work. Most of the time, our role models belong to a privileged group who aren't subjected to the same repercussions; thus, they operate with no fear. I became acutely aware that, whatever the context, the script that works for a privileged group doesn't work for everyone. However, the advice given to those in a not-so-privileged minority works for the majority as well.

I started digging for clues and found some great resources in two books by Linda Babcock and Sara Laschever: *Women Don't Ask* and its follow-up, *Ask for It*. In the second book, the authors cite research that demonstrates clearly that male and female negotiators are perceived differently. When women exhibit aggressive behavior, it does *not* go over well, even though men are forgiven for it or even expected to behave that way (well, that explains my "we'll see" moment). As I started sharpening my skills, through study as well as trial and error, I was more considered in my advice to people who looked like me, and I noticed that the same advice worked just as well for my more privileged audiences. It was as if the advice I started giving myself and other women like me became the on-ramp, while the advice and instruction given to us by male peers was the stairs. Sure, most people can take the stairs, but *everyone* can use the ramp.

CHAPTER 2

THE POWER OF PAUSE

"WHAT ARE YOU GOING TO TEACH ME, LITTLE GIRL?" asked the burly white-haired man.

Another gem in my treasure trove of stories from my early consulting days in the heart of the male-dominated Texas oil and gas industry (either I've developed a more credible vibe or I don't look as young as I used to, because I haven't heard that one in a while—I prefer to think it's the years of honing my craft and not my new wrinkles).

Knowing that a client can lob a doozy like that at any time can be intimidating. That's why I'm not surprised when I hear questions like "But what if they rescind the offer?" "But what if they think I'm greedy?" "But what if I ruin the relationship? How am I going to be able to face them again?" These "but whats" are so common, I can see them coming a mile away, whether from students I meet with during my office hours, or clients negotiating high-stakes scenarios. "But what if it rains while you're out and about?" You carry an umbrella to keep your hair intact. "But what if you get into a car accident?" You wear a seatbelt to prevent serious damage. You can't stay inside forever. You take precautions to mitigate the risks.

I had learned some great lessons from the "fucking bitch" trials, so knowing there was a probability I was going to get harassed or insulted, I had a plan to pause before reacting, take a deep breath and stay calm no matter what. In this "little girl" case, I advised the gentleman caller to "sit tight and you'll find out" (you'll note I refrained from adding "old man"—*that* was a challenge), and he did. We even had a few laughs together later.

The differences in the way men and women are perceived or treated, even when they say the same things, may explain why so many more of the women in my audiences consistently tell me they're afraid to negotiate. It could also explain why, in Linda Babcock's 2003 study, she found that only 7 percent of women surveyed negotiated their salary for their first job after school. Men clocked in at 57 percent, so it seems that many men are also afraid to negotiate.[1]

What's behind all this fear? Why is negotiating so difficult? Let me count the ways:

- perceived threats to our well-being, sense of pride or self-image;
- fear of rejection, or that we might not get what we ask for;
- belief that negotiation has to be a battle, combined with a preference to avoid conflict;
- concern that, instead of being met with rationality, attempts to negotiate will be trampled by the other party's emotions;

- ignorance about the different types of negotiation, and/or an inability to identify what type is being conducted and which strategies are suited to that type;
- failure to charge our negotiation batteries so that we have the power we need;
- lack of understanding of where power comes from and how best to wield it (and when not to wield it);
- inability to adapt our tactics or styles in accordance with who we are and whom we're dealing with (women and men, parents and children, different cultures, etc.);
- ignorance about how to effectively prepare for negotiations;
- poor communication skills.

Thinking your brain might explode? The good news is that we're going to cover solutions for all of the above in the sections to come!

Here's the thing: When the brain senses some type of threat, a lot of stuff happens that makes your heart rate increase, causes your palms to get sweaty and triggers all sorts of other reactions. Going back to our primitive years, perhaps our bodies were bracing us to outrun a predator; today we're running from other threats to our well-being. If you feel that your pride or self-image are being threatened, that could be reason enough to get the blood pumping a little. Fear of rejection? That's a biggie—one of those threats to our well-being. And there is a possibility you won't get your desired outcome if you step outside of your comfort zone and actually ask for something you want. Why do so many romantic comedies depict the male lead as a bumbling fool when he's about to ask the object of his affection out on a date? Fear. Fear of making a mistake. Fear of looking stupid. That potential rejection, or bruised ego, is looming large, and all rational thought goes out the window! Have you ever had those moments where you're in a situation that makes you nervous and you walk away wondering, "Why did I do that!?" or "I should have said . . . " Of course, all common sense returns as soon as you get away from the stressful stimulus.

Why does that even happen? In his book *The Happiness Hypothesis*, Jonathan Haidt describes the emotional, unconscious part of the brain as a large, temperamental elephant, representing our deep emotions, beliefs and desires. It's instinctual. An elephant is freaking strong and goes wherever it wants. The rider sitting on top of the elephant represents the rational side of our brain, the conscious part that analyzes and calculates consequences and outcomes. The rider is positioned to steer the elephant in the most rational or efficient direction to get to the desired destination. But if the rider and elephant disagree, who's going to win that fight: the tiny rider or the six-ton elephant? You experience this all the time when you do things that you know are bad for you—that extra slap of the snooze button, the extra bite of dessert. When rider and elephant are in agreement, life is good, but when they're not, the emotional elephant wins and the rational rider loses—or, even worse, tries to rationalize the less-than-desirable decisions the elephant made. It's the only way to save face when losing the battle to the elephant.

Why am I telling you this? Because I encounter so many people who make the mistake of assuming that negotiating is a rational, unemotional event that is decided solely on spreadsheets, and that everyone's "rider" will be moving in the same direction as their own. After all, people are rational and logical creatures, right? Wrong! We've got elephants running our lives! We're ruled by our emotions, so if you think you can easily appeal to the other party's rider (or even your own) and assume that things will go smoothly, you're going to get trampled by elephants. Another reason why negotiation is so scary for so many.

But what if you could get those emotions under control and get the elephant moving in the same direction as the rider instead of running away? In Babcock's study, those who did negotiate their salaries managed to receive offers that were better by an average of 7.4 percent. That could amount to thousands of dollars a year. Every year. Compounded for many years. Margaret Neale, a professor at the Stanford Graduate School of Business, took the study a step further. She looked at two colleagues joining a company at the same time. Both are offered the same starting salary, but one of them negotiates and receives an extra 7.4 percent. Over the next thirty-five years, they receive identical raises. The employee who didn't negotiate would have to work *an extra eight years* to end up with the same total income as the one who did. I don't know about you, but I love my job, and I would *still* like to retire eight years earlier!

What if you could train yourself to pause that overactive fear center in your brain and get your elephant to stay put, allowing that rational rider to take over when needed? Well, you can! Feeling nervous about that salary negotiation? Pause. Consider the story you read that sounded exactly like your situation! Feeling powerless before you go into that important meeting? Pause. Recall all of the things you read in the Power section that you can leverage to gain some confidence. Don't know what to say when they say no? Pause. Remember those questions you learned in the Communication section. Each insight you collect is a tool for your rider to keep that elephant calm and heading onto the on-ramp instead of getting stuck at the stairs.

When you pause to get your fear under control, you can start chipping away at retiring a few years early. You can solve problems with your partner at home without worrying about it leading to divorce. You can even prevent a temper tantrum from that little one who you're worried may cause a scene. Your wealth and your sanity are in the palm of your hand . . . if you can take a calming breath and find the mental pause button first.

CHAPTER 3

REDEFINING NEGOTIATION

WE IDENTIFIED REASONS WHY FEAR IS SO OFTEN TRIG-
gered when people hear the word *negotiation*, but the most common one is that people misunderstand the definition. They assume
that every negotiation is like stepping into a boxing ring or some
other form of combat. I can assure you I have never had to take a
swing at anyone with whom I've negotiated. And neither have any
of my clients. Feel better?

The definition of *negotiation* is this: the process by which two (or
more) people reach an agreement. That's all it is. And yet our emotional elephants go berserk thinking there's more to it. Your first
step is to consider this basic definition. It's actually quite positive
when you pause to reflect on it. The aim is agreement—not abuse.
Not everyone will get that, so part of your job as an effective negotiator is to use the skills outlined in this book to get them to see it that
way. The agreement may not be everyone's cup of tea, but it's going
to be something they can live with.

Starting with this perspective on the purpose of negotiation will
undoubtedly help your mindset. It will also affect how much or how

little your emotions take over and how others respond to you. In his book *Never Split the Difference,* ex-FBI hostage negotiator Christopher Voss succinctly observes that "negotiation is not an act of battle; it is a process of discovery." An excellent illustration of shifting the mindset to get your emotions under control.

The next step in getting your emotions under control is learning about the various types of negotiations. You probably already have some sense of what's appropriate in different circumstances; for instance, you wouldn't treat a negotiations at the car dealership the way you would one with your boss. And a negotiation with a souvenir vendor while you're on vacation is going to look and sound different than one with your long-term client. Haggling with your client the way you would with that souvenir vendor could result in the loss of that client. Thus, it's important to pause to consider, "What type of negotiation am I dealing with?"

There are so many types of negotiations, it's hard to know where to begin. To make it a little easier, most practitioners and academics lump them into two broad categories: competitive or collaborative negotiations.

Competitive negotiations are those that are carried out with a win/lose mentality, fueled by a fear of scarcity. These negotiations typically center around money or some other commodity. It doesn't get more competitive than haggling over cash. Everyone wants it. What you take, I lose, and vice versa, so we have to compete to get the most. If it's scarce, I want it and I want it *now*. I'm not thinking about long-term repercussions or such intangibles as risk, security or relationships. If I'm in a competitive negotiation, my objective is to get the most I can and get it quickly. Because these negotiations are all about me, with little to no concern about the other party, I refer to them as **My Way** negotiations.

Collaborative negotiations are those in which each party considers the other party's wants or needs in addition to their own. Money is just one of many factors that are at stake. We're thinking about total *value*, meaning issues other than cash that are worth something to one of the parties—we might even call some of them priceless. For example, can you assign a dollar value to job security? What about the factors that contribute to your health or stress levels? Maybe your boss couldn't possibly pay you enough to stay late at the office because the ability to tuck in your kids at night is too important to you to put a price tag on it. The conversations to explore these values are going to look and sound different than those focused on cash. After all, you're going to have to deal with that boss over and over again, so you do have to be concerned about long-term consequences. Now, instead of *me*, you have to be more concerned with *we*. If I'm going to be dealing with you again, then it's not about win/lose; I'll have to have some concern for you and our collective experience. Now I've got to consider **Our Way** instead of My Way.

COLLABORATIVE	COMPETITIVE
Warm and congenial	Cold and impersonal
Many variables, making discussions more complex	Focused heavily on price, with few other variables

COLLABORATIVE	COMPETITIVE
Some information is exchanged to build the trust required to have involved conversations	Secretive about information that could be used against us
Longer-term focus; thus, we may need to deal with the other party and/or consequences for an extended period	Transactional, short-term focus; little concern for consequences to relationships
Being mindful of relationships and the interests of all parties, hence, Our Way	Looking out for your own interest with little regard for the other party, hence, My Way

COLLABORATIVE OR COMPETITIVE? HOW DO YOU KNOW?

Even though we've managed to carve out these two broad types of negotiations, we have to acknowledge that, like most things in life, negotiation is not purely black and white. The brain and human behavior are complex, and people will behave differently under certain circumstances. And few negotiations are 100 percent Our Way or My Way. There are many shades of gray, and it's rare that you're at one extreme or the other. It's no wonder people tell me they're exhausted after a negotiation.

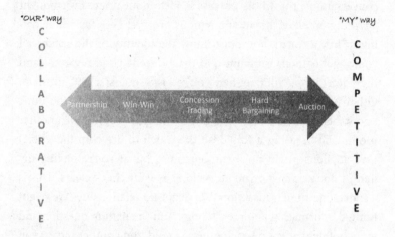

Figure 1: The negotiation spectrum. On the competitive, darker side you'll find the types of negotiations that are self-focused—that is, with a focus on **My Way**. The collaborative, lighter side of negotiation includes the types of negotiations that are focused on mutual benefit, or **Our Way**.

The spectrum in figure 1 is a visual representation of the gradual progression from competitive to collaborative negotiations. Let's work our way across the spectrum, starting with the dark, competitive side.

AUCTIONS

Imagine the dark side being as cold and impersonal as possible (like the heart of the wicked witch in every Disney movie). An auction is a prime example of this extreme. At a live auction, you don't have conversations; the whole process is just about price. Ever bought anything on eBay? It's an anonymous process. Let's say you're trying to buy a watch. You don't know the identity of the seller—all you've got is their username and maybe some good reviews—and they don't know yours either; you're just "superstar999" to them. Other people could be bidding on the same watch, but you don't know them either. (For all you know, the seller could have another profile and be using it to bid on the watch to drive up the price.) Live auctions might not be anonymous, but if you're buying my item, I don't care who you are as long as your check clears. This is a short, one-time transaction. We've got no relationship. We've got limited information about each other and the item in question and we're not dependent on each other. I could find another buyer; you could find another watch. The only thing we have to discuss is the cost. There are no guarantees, warranties or future deals to take into account—it's all anonymous, after all!

Outside of cash, another situation that you could find yourself negotiating is when you're trying to fight for space on a crowded bus. You may do it without even uttering a word, negotiating solely with your body language (to be discussed later), but space is a scarce commodity on public transportation and you're trying to make yourself comfortable with little concern for the complete strangers around you.

HARD BARGAINING

Moving along the spectrum, hard bargaining is similar to the auction in that money is still the main factor, but we may have a few other, lower-priority items to firm up. If you're buying a used car, for example, your primary concern is going to be the price. You may decide to find out about some extra bells and whistles, like some oil changes or floor mats, but they are not going to be the deal breakers or high priorities. It's still about trying to get *my* way on price and everything else. You're not looking out for the salesperson's best interests. And for those who are thinking, "But I don't want to screw him over," the salesman wouldn't sell the car to you if it was going to cost him his job. *He's* the one responsible for following his company rules.

CONCESSION TRADING

In concession trading, you give the other party something, but only if you get something in return—and what you give them has some value to you. Price may be a factor, but often there are plenty of non-monetary items that drive the give and take in this zone on the spectrum. You may see this type of negotiating more frequently at home with children. Though it sometimes has to do with the exchange of money, it more often sounds like this: "If you clean the garage, then I'll give you a ride to the mall."

Concessions can also come in the form of small compromises, where each person has to give up a little something in the exchange. Kids practice this stuff all the time. My nieces are constantly negotiating for use of their toys.

Overheard in my living room:

> **Child A:** I want to play with the Nintendo Switch [or whatever the toy of the moment may be].

Child B: You can have it for five minutes.

Child A: [whining] But you've had it for such a long time! I want a longer turn.

Child B: Okay. If you give me some of your chocolate, you can have it for ten minutes.

Then the negotiation continues as they discuss how much chocolate to exchange for how many additional minutes. They've both conceded something (time or food) and they've both gained something in return.

WIN-WIN

As we move from the "me" to the "we" side of the spectrum, buzzwords like "win-win" start showing up. This type is just what it sounds like: agreements that both parties benefit from, with no need for any compromise or feeling of loss. No chocolate or video game deprivation is required. Thinking back to my nieces, if one needed to get rid of her chocolate because it was making her sick, and the other was looking for someone to take care of her video game for a few minutes while she stepped away, they'd be poised for a win-win.

One of the mistakes I see from extremely collaborative negotiators is the belief that every negotiation is a win-win. Sometimes the other party just doesn't have it in them, or the circumstances don't permit, for both of you to get everything you want out of the situation. As per my example above, how often does anyone *need* to get rid of their chocolate? Of course, for those who are super-competitive and love the chance to "beat" the other party, their mistake is that they fail to see the opportunity for a win-win and see everything as win-lose. There's no thought about the "we," and they live their negotiation lives with blinders on, limiting their view of what's possible.

Win-wins happen all around us. Sometimes you don't even realize that you're negotiating them. My nieces and I share a love of Oreo cookies and my mother keeps her pantry stocked at all times, so when we all congregate at my parents' home, we raid her stash. You would think that her supply would be rapidly depleted, but here's the thing: my nieces love the chocolate biscuits and I only eat the creamy centers (don't judge me). Because I have two nieces and Oreos come with two biscuits, I would call that a win-win-win. Or it could be a win-win-win-win, since my mother doesn't have to buy any additional cookies. Life is good.

It seems like a lot of my examples are about food, so here's a different situation for you. Let's say your employer is considering cost-cutting measures and realizes that office real estate is the expense category with the most potential room for savings. At the same time, you are getting sick of commuting into work and having to spend *soooo* much time sitting in traffic when you could easily be working on your laptop at home—in your pajamas. So, you approach your boss to see if there's any way you can spend less time in the office and spend more time working from home. This is a situation I've seen quite a bit in recent years, and both the employers and employees are happy to minimize costs, while increasing productivity and quality of life in this win-win scenario. Both parties have their financial and qualitative needs met, with no downside. That's an Our Way solution.

PARTNERSHIPS

When you get to the most collaborative end of the spectrum, words like *partnership* come up. You'd think it must be all wine and roses over here, since win-win sounded so great. Not so fast. This type of negotiation can be great, but it can also get messy. I remember having a client once tell me, "We don't call the people we work with our 'customers'; we call them our 'partners.'" Oh boy.

Here's the thing about partnerships: they are the closest of relationships. They involve two parties who are dependent on one another and who would do something at their own expense for the sake of the partnership because of said dependency. Sometimes you've got to take a hit because if the other party goes down, they're dragging you down with them, whether they mean to or not.

Marriage is certainly a partnership scenario that comes to mind in everyday life. Because you're thinking about the long-term *our* way, sometimes you do things for your spouse for the sake of the partnership, even if you don't like them. Short-term pain for long-term gain. Maybe it's agreeing to visit your in-laws over the holidays because you know it will make your spouse happy, thus allowing you to avoid endless arguments, or perhaps even because you know your spouse will suffer through the same fate next year, when you ask them to join your parents—and aunts and uncles and cousins—on vacation.

In the business world these partnership situations are less frequent. Many people have a romantic idea that everyone will partner with them, but most businesses are out there to meet their own needs—their one and only priority—in a My Way fashion. There are a lot of folks who will make it look like an Our Way negotiation, only to fail to follow through on the part that benefits you. They're like wolves in sheep's clothing. Any agreement you reach with them might seem great until you find out you're getting eaten alive.

When partnerships do truly exist, sometimes they can get ugly, but both sides stay partnered out of necessity. In September 2007[2] the Toronto Transit Commission (TTC) announced it was looking to replace its aging fleet of streetcars. In April 2009, after nearly two years of negotiating with suppliers, the TTC made a deal with Bombardier for $1.2 billion to deliver 204 vehicles to the city. The first streetcar was delivered for testing in September 2012, with the rest to flow in stages until the last were to be delivered by 2018.

From that point on a series of unfortunate and poorly planned events transpired. In the first year of testing, the TTC's CEO at the time deemed the new streetcars so poorly manufactured that the agency wouldn't take possession of them until they were fixed (keep in mind that these new cars were expected to last longer than Toronto's existing fleet, which was more than thirty years old). A few years later there were still so many issues that Bombardier had to invest in operational and quality assurance processes at its facilities in Mexico and Thunder Bay, Ontario. Then there was a strike. And parts shortages. It was no surprise when the announcement came at the end of 2014 that the manufacturer was behind schedule, having delivered only *three* of the forty-three streetcars it had been slated to deliver that year. After a reminder that the TTC would invoke the penalty clauses in the contract should the 2018 deadline not be met, Bombardier agreed to deliver more frequently, projecting that thirty vehicles would be delivered by the end of 2015 . . . which actually happened at the end of 2016 (by which time there were supposed to be a hundred).

Do you see where this is going? In October 2015 Bombardier admitted it was dealing with more manufacturing problems. In the meantime, Toronto riders were experiencing service reductions and shortages because the aging fleet couldn't handle the demand. The TTC temporarily put buses into service on streetcar routes, but they were no match for the volume of people the TTC was relying on the new, larger streetcars to move, which meant riders like me were waiting forever to get on board. On October 28, 2015, the TTC decided to sue Bombardier for at least $50 million to cover its costs. In April 2019 it settled for an undisclosed amount. All the while, the two sides were continuing their business partnership!

The TTC had been spending out of pocket to deal with the service gaps the delivery delays caused, and it's unlikely that the settlement covered all of its losses. Bombardier had already invested $20 million in its facilities to meet demand, and had to pay more because of the settlement—a clear example of having to do something at your own expense for the sake of the partnership. At the TTC's board meeting on October 24, 2019, Bombardier was still sixteen streetcars shy of its target, and the company revealed it had lost money on the contract. It turns out that customizing streetcars for Toronto streets was not as easy as expected.

You may be thinking, "Why didn't the TTC just pull out and find another supplier years ago?" And that would be a rational thought. This deal started in 2009, with an expectation that all of the streetcars would be in service by 2018. That's nine years. Prior to letting out the contract, the TTC spent two years finding the right supplier and ironing out the details of the deal. So, if the TTC had pulled out at any point in the process—say, in 2015—to find a new supplier, assuming they didn't also run into legal issues over cancelling the contract, it would have had to deal with another two-year search and prototype-development process, followed by however many years it would take to build and deliver the 150 or so streetcars it was short. Maybe the agency would have an entire fleet by 2025, give or take a couple years? The bottom line: there would've been a further delay and additional risk. If the new supplier had run into problems, it could've forced the TTC to wait even longer for its streetcars.

That's the problem with long-term negotiations such as these: you sometimes have to do something at your own expense for the sake of the partnership. The TTC suffered through service delays and temporary deployment of buses to make things work so that Bombardier could finish the contract. The agency wasn't happy about it, but was so dependent on the other party that it had to make do; the alternative was so ugly, it was difficult to walk away despite being unhappy. Bombardier also couldn't walk away. The company already looked bad to investors and potential customers, but imagine how much worse its reputation would be if it were known as the company that walked away from projects.

Unlike this corporate debacle, many partnerships do entail more positive interactions overall. Marriage (a healthy one, at least) is a prime example. Spouses are constantly negotiating with one another. And one partner will often do something at their own expense for the sake of the partnership, knowing that it will prove to be worthwhile in the long term. Whether the concessions include taking turns making sacrifices for one another on movie or restaurant choices or where the kids will go to school, the ups will outweigh the downs, making the partnership viable. Otherwise, well, you're going to slide across the spectrum to the "me" negotiations that are divorce proceedings.

No matter what your situation, your negotiation skills will definitely be useful. Just make sure you know where on the spectrum it's appropriate to be operating. In the next chapter, we'll discuss the factors that will help you identify that all-important location.

CHAPTER 4

WHERE AM I ON THE SPECTRUM?

IT'S NOT ALWAYS OBVIOUS, ESPECIALLY IF YOU'RE NEW to the conversation about negotiating, what type of scenario you're looking at or how to handle it. But it's important to determine where the situation sits on the spectrum, because that will allow you to open up a world of potential value, avoid making costly mistakes and protect yourself from more competitive negotiators.

In this chapter, we'll look at the key factors that help to determine an opportunity's position on the negotiation spectrum: time, information, complexity and creativity, trust and relationships.

TIME

How long is this discussion expected to last? How long will I be dealing with the outcome of this negotiation? Is this a quick transaction that's going to be over in minutes, after which I never hear from the other party again, or is this a longer-running discussion with consequences that could last for weeks, months or years?

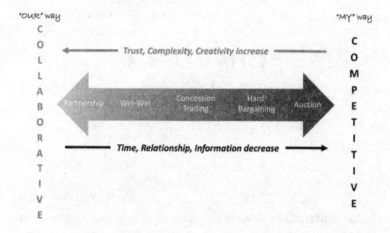

Figure 2: The negotiation spectrum. Factors like trust, complexity, creativity, time, relationships and information help us to determine whether we are dealing with a more competitive My Way negotiation or a more collaborative Our Way negotiation.

When you're buying a pair of elephant pants at a market in Thailand, you don't expect to do future business with the vendor, nor do you expect to have a warranty on your pants that lasts any longer than the instant the cash leaves your hands. You're not concerned about any damage to your reputation, and you're not worried about building trust with this person. If you're buying those pants online in an eBay auction, the negotiation that might have taken minutes on a beach in Thailand could take seconds from the comfort of your couch. And good luck trying to make contact with that seller again; they could close up shop the moment your transaction is complete.

When you don't have much time to complete the agreement and there's not much to consider in terms of long-term repercussions, it's a safe bet that you're in a basic negotiation, typically involving something scarce like cash (or chocolate, if you're negotiating with my nieces). And if the other party is trying to impose a (likely artificial) deadline, then you're clearly on the darkest, most competitive side of the spectrum. Brace yourself for them to operate in My Way mode.

If getting a deal done is going to take multiple discussions and you have to consider long-term effects, you've got a different type of negotiation on your hands—one that is more complex, with more variables in the mix (which is why all those discussions are needed) and other factors to bear in mind (those pesky long-term repercussions). When the transaction itself takes days, weeks, months or even years to complete (I've been involved in all of the above), there will be a whole whack of other complicated issues to consider, and the situation will require you to open up your perspective to some Our Way negotiation considerations.

INFORMATION

When you're involved in those quick, one-dimensional discussions, you don't have much information to go on. When scarcity is at the core of the discussion (whether you're negotiating for cash, chocolate, beans or some other seemingly scarce commodity), no one wants to start sharing their secrets. For example, when you talk to the person selling pants in the market, you are rarely compelled to say, "I have $20 in my pocket; feel free to keep harassing me until you get all of it." You don't want them to know how much you've got, just as they don't want you to know they would be willing to let the pants go for $10 less than their asking price. They also don't want to tell you the raw material costs, or that they were just about to throw the pants in the garbage since they've been trying to get rid of them for months and they're taking up too much space on their truck. Any of that information would give the other party leverage, and if this is a competitive My Way negotiation, you don't want to give anyone any power over you.

On the other hand, if we are dealing with an Our Way negotiation, we need to know a little bit more about each other and what motivates us. If we're negotiating over where to go for dinner, then I might want to tell you about my nut allergy so that we don't hit up the new plant-based restaurant (I've been told by one restaurant in particular to stay the hell away or I will die). Trust me: the last thing you want is to spend your evening riding in the back of the ambulance with me instead of enjoying the ambience of some other desirable restaurant. Equally, you may want to tell me that you don't like spicy food so that we don't end up at an Indian restaurant where you'll be eating only naan bread all night. See how sharing information works here? It's in our interests to divulge some information to make sure we find a solution that meets both of our needs.

When the negotiations get even more complex, we have even more to unpack about what to share and what to hold back. Generally, as you move along the spectrum from "me" to "we" negotiations, it gets safer and more beneficial to share more information. As your negotiations get more complex, sharing your preferences or ranking of the issues involved is safe, but sharing how you would weight them (that is, how deeply important they are) is a no-no. Telling someone, "If I had to rank them, schedule flexibility, compensation and vacation time would be my top three issues in order of importance" can help the other party to decide how to expend their energy in finding a viable solution for you. Telling them, "Vacation is really a 'nice-to-have,' but it's way less important than anything I've mentioned" could result in their dismissing that request altogether. What you share and how you share it become tricky as you decide how much you trust the other party to use the information for mutual benefit as opposed to using it to take advantage of you. We'll build on this in later sections.

COMPLEXITY AND CREATIVITY

Naturally, when all you're talking about is how much cash or how many beans you're willing to trade, the discussion will be scarce and secretive, as is customary on the dark side of the spectrum. As more issues are added into the mix, the situation gets more complex. It's like juggling. If you're juggling only one ball, it's easy to transfer it from one hand to the other. Start adding balls and it takes a lot more work and coordination to make sure you're not dropping any. The same is true of negotiation. When you open up the discussion to more issues, it gets more complex and takes more energy to manage. In addition to deciding how much information to share, more analysis is required to figure out how much value needs to be created and which issues are more important to whom. There are also more options for trades, in an assortment of permutations. Tracking all of that gets thorny, not just because there are so many issues being discussed, but also because so many of them are based on more than basic math. We start discussing qualitative issues like guarantees, quality of life and stress levels.

Take, for example, a job offer negotiation. Most people immediately think of the salary that's going to be discussed, but you are missing SO MUCH VALUE if you go in with that narrow perspective. Throw some other balls into the juggling act. It's more work, but it's so much more entertaining and valuable. The ability to have flexible hours or even work from home could make a bigger impact on your wallet than a few extra bucks that are going to be subject to taxes. That's not to say that I don't believe in going after every single dollar you can, but money is one of those win-lose issues that evokes the scarcity mentality in both parties. Applying some more creative thought can be an easier route to wealth. Factor in how much less those days working from home will cost you in transit, or the extra time your kids need to be in daycare because of those hours of commuting (not to mention the intangible value of saving your sanity by avoiding traffic and getting a few extra minutes of sleep—I live in Toronto, where getting anywhere takes forever and creates a lot of frustration). Having the company cover cell phone bills and related expenses is another way to maintain your bank account balance while allowing the company to spend less.

Do you have to move for a new job? In that case, a signing bonus could help you with first and last month's rent for your new place, or with new furniture that you don't have to charge to your credit card and start paying interest on. Making sure the company covers your moving costs could be even better. Let's say your move costs $10,000. Assuming a marginal income tax rate of 40 percent, every extra dollar you make will have forty cents taken away, so you've got only sixty cents to spend on your movers. That means you'll need to get your new employer to give you $16,666.66 so that, after your 40 percent is taken away for taxes, you've got the necessary funds for the movers. Or you could get your new employers to pay the movers directly, and they can spend $10,000 instead of $16,666.66 from their recruitment fund. Sounds like a win-win opportunity.

But what about the stuff that doesn't have a tangible value? How about a great title that's going to give you access to career- and résumé-building networking? The promise of limited travel so that you've got one less thing to juggle at home? Or maybe the opportunity to travel so you can see the world on someone else's dime—and even tack on vacation, thus shrinking your vacation spending? What about the joy that comes with working on projects that excite you or working for mentors you look forward to learning from every day? There are so many things you can negotiate that can't necessarily be valued with a price tag. These are the issues that will help you manage your stress once the mortgage is paid and food is on the table. They're what will keep you from quitting and having to spend late nights on the computer, starting your job search all over again. That's quality of life.

Of course, in order to find agreement on these qualitative issues, you need to take the time to have meaningful discussions and ask for information that's going to help you discover some of the other balls that can be thrown into the juggling mix. You'll also have to consider what information you'll need to share in order to help your new boss identify what would be valuable to you. In these types of negotiations, we often talk about "growing the pie." The pie is the amount of value to go around. A bigger pie means greater value for everyone to share. How can you make a bigger pie if neither of you knows what to put in it? Making pies isn't easy. It's complex. If creativity isn't your strong suit, then try to encourage the other party to get creative by asking questions or even holding a brainstorming session—the ultimate in information-sharing. The more issues that are in the mix, the more complexity is involved, the more you move toward Our Way negotiations on the lighter side of the spectrum. You can see the light when you start adding issues for discussion!

Not everyone has the will or the ability to see the light. I see this all the time in the corporate world. Some people just get tunnel vision. Sometimes they're not as capable as you are, but your creative skill rubs off on them, and your ability can lure them from the dark side of the spectrum to the light side. Other times, no matter how hard you try to toss those creative ideas around, the other party just keeps shutting them down, stuck in their dark tunnel. Part of being an effective negotiator is recognizing where the best possible outcome lies; if the other party is not capable of moving along the spectrum with you, you maximize the opportunity on the darker side of it.

TRUST

As you juggle more and more issues, you've got to get more creative and resourceful to keep them all in the air. Once you get past the basic issues like money, there are all sorts of things that can create value for all parties involved. Efficiency, security, guarantees and ease of execution are all elements that often have nothing to do with money. In order to have open conversations about how to create this type of value, you each need to be comfortable enough to open up and share what could create some of these interesting sources of value. The only way to do that is with trust.

A Dutch colleague once shared a proverb with me, explaining that "trust arrives on foot and leaves on horseback." Trust takes a long time to build and can be broken in a flash. Once broken, it takes even longer to repair (if it can be repaired at all). We can build trust in baby steps: acknowledging the other person's feelings or contributions, showing concern for their well-being, sharing a piece of information (even if it's something they already know). This perception of concern for the other party often results in the reciprocation of these gestures. This, in turn, leads to much more interesting discussions and identification of new sources of value for both parties.

I once had a client ask me for a proposal for some consulting and training work for his team. It was a logistics company that had a lot of customer service staff spending time on the phone, negotiating quick contracts with trucking and storage service providers. Their negotiations usually lasted less than a minute. I spent some time in the office observing the team, gave them some suggestions on techniques and tools they could use to improve their deals, and then provided a proposal for a customized training program. The client reviewed it and asked, "How would you like to make more money?" I was intrigued. He proposed a risk/reward program in which he would give me a percentage of my fee upfront, and if the team improved its profitability in the month following the program, he would pay me the remainder of my fee along with a bit extra.

It was a creative idea that became complex to carry out. We spoke at length about how the company measured profitability and what could affect it. Increased profitability depended largely on the team members striking better deals with the trucking companies they were speaking to, but there were other, unpredictable factors as well. Gas prices fluctuated constantly; a strike could make transport prices skyrocket; an unexpected event like a frozen crop of oranges could suddenly make a lot of trucks available, at lower prices. I had a hard time wrapping my head around the proposal in a way that made me sure I wouldn't be adversely affected by conditions that were beyond my control; at the same time, I asked the company about conditions that might make it seem more profitable than could realistically be attributed to my training. By looking out for the client's well-being, I was demonstrating trust. And by being so transparent with all of the data they track to monitor the trends in the areas I mentioned, they demonstrated it right back to me.

We ended up agreeing to a handsome fee for me if the team hit its profit targets. We did this even though I'd already told the client that if it wasn't pleased with the results, I would come back and spend more hands-on time in the office with the team to guarantee that the company had made a great investment. The client took comfort in knowing that my entire business was based on referrals (I didn't even have a website until my fourth year in business, and even that was terrible). Thanks to the trust between us, we were able to openly discuss options that would protect both of our interests. Not only did we land on a greater upfront percentage of my fee, as well as a greater overall increase in my fee, but we agreed on a formula for success and a backup plan if the benchmarks weren't reached.

Without some trust between us, the client wouldn't have been so forthcoming about the patterns and trends in its business and its industry. That would make any conversations about additional value and profit-sharing impossible—going into an agreement blindly would be foolish for me. The more information we had to play with, the more options for value we could create to grow the pie between us. That sort of complexity and creativity is possible because of the trust that's created between parties. The more of it we have, the more information we have about what can go into the pie to create that greater value.

RELATIONSHIPS

The more comfortable we feel opening up (with minimal fear of being exploited), the more creative opportunities abound. As we move along that spectrum from the dark side to the light, more information flows (both ways) and trust builds. The connection between the parties gets stronger as the trust increases. The longer it takes to complete the discussion, or the longer-lasting its conse-quences, the more there is at stake and the greater the connection between the parties will be. We've established that quick one-off transactions, like auctions and buying vacation souvenirs, don't involve dependencies or long-term repercussions. The connection or relationship between the parties there is brief and weak, and there is no need to foster it any further.

But if you're a florist selling to a soon-to-be bride, the transaction *could* happen quickly, or it could take a couple of consultations. If you get a deposit upfront and receive the rest of the funds on the day of the wedding, which is weeks or months later, that transaction won't be completed for a while. There are also some longer-range repercussions—if you hope the transaction results in referrals or positive online reviews. So, this situation is a little farther over into the gray zone. This doesn't mean you'll be consulting with this person on other client requests or taking them on as a business partner, so don't kid yourself about how much farther along the spectrum you're moving. It's not as though you're going to start sharing information about your raw material costs and suppliers, and it's not as though you'll be the bride's new best friend, chowing down on wedding cake at the end of the night. But you do have some kind of relationship or connection, even if it's just a cordial business transaction.

Because now there are some possible consequences (good or bad) to the interaction, there is a certain level of dependency between the two parties. The bride depends on the florist to make sure the flower arrangements appear as promised. When the florist blocks the time in his calendar and orders supplies, he becomes dependent on the bride to follow through on the order and pay him accordingly. He may also be depending on receiving a good review online or having the bride refer her friends to him. All of these possibilities carry different levels of dependency. If the florist is so busy that he doesn't have time for any more clients, then those referrals don't mean anything, and if he has five-star ratings from hundreds of other reviewers, maybe there is no worry about a single review bringing down the average. Dependency is thus gone. The florist has no future worries, and no further contact will be required once this job is done, which means there is no relationship, or a weak one at best.

In a sharing economy, the reason we're willing to trust a complete stranger by getting in their car or staying in their home is that we've created dependency and a longer-lasting relationship with the review and rating systems on platforms like Uber and Airbnb. That dependency on a good review (on both sides) forces a little more trust between the two sides. I used to host Airbnb guests in my basement apartment. I would send complete strangers a code to a lockbox outside the house that contained a key to get into the basement. Most of the time I never even met the people who were coming and going in my home. I didn't feel the need to, because I knew that most folks want to be able to continue using the platform, so screwing things up by abusing me and my space would earn them a negative review, causing other potential hosts to deny their requests. Of course, it wasn't in *my* best interest to give guests a suboptimal stay because I needed them to leave me a positive review if I hoped to ever host anyone again.

This scenario presumes, of course, that we both intended to continue using the system. If one of us decided we didn't care to participate anymore, there would be no more dependence on good feedback, and therefore no basis for relationships and trust. If a host or a guest doesn't care about future reviews, they can screw the other party over. To minimize the risk of that happening, I only hosted guests with positive reviews, banking on the safe assumption that they would want to maintain their reputations.

I wouldn't rent the space to people who were booking on behalf of someone else (such as a parent renting for a kid with no user profile), because that would leave me vulnerable to a breakdown in the dependency, the severity of which I couldn't assess. These transactions were about more than cash; they were about the level of courtesy from guests—following my house rules about smoking and not making excessive noise or damaging my furnishings. After all, I was living upstairs, and the value of minimizing my stress was super-important to me.

For a hotel, the review system is one-sided: guests can leave negative reviews online, which downgrades the hotel's reputation; but guests don't get reviewed by hotel staff, so their personal reputations are not at risk. To lengthen the transaction just a little and create some dependency, the hotel keeps a credit card number on file for deposits. In doing so, they take the negotiation from the dark zone to one that is slightly more gray. It fosters a little more civility between hotel employees and guests, because each side is now accountable to the other. This creates a nominally stronger relationship, or connection, between the parties and creates a bit more trust.

When you're dealing with someone like your child's teacher, lashing out at them may not be your best move; your dealings with them are not the same as your dealings with that souvenir vendor, from whom you can just walk away, never to see them again. Not only would you be denying your child a chance to start learning how to self-advocate, but it's also likely that you will have multiple interactions with the teacher over the course of the school year (and potentially beyond). You are somewhat dependent on them to make sure your kid has a positive educational experience. And they depend on you to make sure their school year doesn't become a nightmare. There's definitely some Our Way benefit in this scenario for both parties, even if it may seem at first that your negotiation involves something simple, like whether or not your kid will get to sing a solo in the spring concert.

As we move toward the lighter side of the spectrum, the relationships get stronger and that interdependency increases. If you and your partner are trying to decide where you should spend your annual vacation, that decision will have some long-term repercussions. If you treat it like a My Way negotiation, you'll likely be dealing with some serious resentment and possible passive-aggressive behavior from them, leading up to and even during the vacation. In fact, that resentment could last well beyond the vacation. Prepare to hear the words "we did your thing last time" during your next negotiation. All of that sounds counter to the purpose of a vacation, which is to de-stress. Treating your negotiation with someone on whom your personal well-being depends as a My Way negotiation is clearly problematic. You need to work things through in a collaborative way or you'll be dealing with the fallout for a long time. Some methods of negotiating collaboratively are coming in the section on communication.

THE SPECTRUM IN ACTION

I have done a ton of work in the retail and manufacturing industries. Time and again, I've watched retail giants behave in a My Way approach full of arbitrary deadlines, threats and attempts to keep

the negotiations focused solely on a transfer of cash from the supplier's bank account to their own. It usually sounds something like
"Give me your products cheaper, with no strings attached, or I'm
going to take all of them off our shelves." In a market where Ama-
zon has turned retailers' worlds upside down, everything is available at the click of a mouse and quarterly profits are reported to
The Street, everyone is focused on the short term. They want their
money and they want it quickly. And desperate times call for desperate My Way measures, even if it doesn't make any rational sense
in the medium term. Manufacturers usually call me in a panic when
they think they're on the brink of losing one of these high-stakes
negotiations. I say "losing" intentionally here because the retailer is
treating the negotiation like a competitive, My Way scenario. The
retailer has been making my client feel like they are insignificant,
easily replaced at any time with a competitor—or even their own
store brand.[3]

One client I worked with was engaged in a negotiation with one
of the largest retailers in the world and asked for my help to close a
multiyear contract with them. My client's popular household product, which they wanted to keep on the retailer's shelves for at least a
few more years, was the leading product in its category by far. The
retailer had been dropping hints that it would consider developing its
own product, leading the supplier to believe there was no dependency
whatsoever—the retailer could seemingly live without that relationship and drop the product at any moment. Technically, it was true.
Any retailer can remove a product from its shelves at any time—but
not without consequences. If it's a product you're loyal to, like Oreos
(just to be clear, this particular story is not about Oreo cookies; in

all of the anecdotes in this book, the names have been changed), the store-brand replacement just isn't going to cut it, and you'll start shopping somewhere else to get your hands on your beloved cookies. The retailer that dropped the item may regret its decision.

Knowing that my client's product enjoyed some of the highest customer loyalty scores in the market, and that shoppers were certain to go elsewhere to get it, my task was to help my client make sure that the retailer—let's call them Global Retailer (GR)—knew this. We reinforced the relationship between the two businesses by reminding the retailer that the product needed to be on its shelves if it hoped to keep its customers happy. That reminder convinced GR to play a little nicer and be a little less extreme in its list of demands. It even started considering more creative solutions than what amounted to a ransom note.

Now, you may be thinking, "But how could GR really need that one product? They sell billions of dollars' worth of other items. Surely they're not *that* dependent on these guys." The fact is, the buyers at GR's head office who have to deal with the lost sales in their department, and report on that loss to their bosses and their bosses' shareholders, are definitely dependent on that one item. The relationship is between people, after all, and these people needed to work together, whether they liked it or not, to keep sales and profits high.

Bringing this all back together, you want to *pause* to consider where you are on the spectrum so that you don't make the mistake of investing too much or too little effort in the negotiation at hand. Ask yourself some of the following questions (some of which may apply to multiple categories):

TIME

- Will this transaction be completed quickly, with few consequences?
- Will it require a few meetings or conversations to work out the details of what's at stake?
- Is there a chance of retaliation, or are you never going to see or hear from these people again?

INFORMATION

- How much do you truly know about the circumstances?
- Has the other party shared any information with you, or are they being secretive?
- Do you have enough information to figure out what else could create value here?
- Is it worth the effort to analyze and find other options?
- Do you sense that you can trust the other party enough to share any information about what could create value for you?

COMPLEXITY AND CREATIVITY

- Is the other party capable of creative thought?
- Will the other side be open to creative solutions if you put them out there?
- Is this only about money, or is the transaction more complex than that?

TRUST AND RELATIONSHIPS
- How dependent are you on each other?
- Will you have to deal with one another again, or is this a one-and-done transaction?
- What do you want your relationship to be?

All of these questions and more will help you determine what to expect and how to handle any given negotiation. The answers will help you to figure out where the best opportunities exist, and how much time and effort will be required to secure them. They'll set the tone for the solutions that will serve you best—or potentially serve both of you. They can help you determine what the other party is capable of, and what you need to do to take care of your own needs. Maybe you're treating this as a "we" negotiation when all they've got in them is "me," and if that's the case, you could end up being exploited.

So, pause to reflect on the circumstances. Pause to consider the possibilities. Pause to figure out what it will take to move the other party to the end of the spectrum that's going to get you what you want. These fundamentals are the first steps to your success.

PAUSE FOR REFLECTION

SECTION 1 | BREAKING DOWN THE BASICS
CHECKLIST OF KEY TAKEAWAYS

✓ **One size does not fit all.** Remember to consider that your voice may sound different than those around you. Consider your specific circumstances before you mimic someone else. The same script could be received differently depending on the context. We'll explore this even more in subsequent sections.

✓ **Our emotions can be a lot stronger than our rational thought when we're under stress.** Because of fear, your rider is going to have a hard time controlling the emotional elephant. And even when you get good at controlling it, other riders may not be moving in the same direction. Those emotional elephants are often leading the charge, so don't assume everyone is going to be rational.

✓ **Different types of negotiations require different sets of strategies and behaviors.** You wouldn't treat your partner in a "we" negotiation the same way you would a one-time vendor in a "me" negotiation. Know what type of negotiation you're dealing with, and treat it accordingly.

✓ **Pause to consider the various factors that help you determine where you are—or could be—on the spectrum.** Time, information, complexity and creativity, trust and relationships. These factors will help you determine what to expect and how to handle whatever comes your way. You'll be able to identify the best opportunities and determine how much time and effort are required to secure them.

SECTION 2

POWER ISN'T ALWAYS OBVIOUS

CHAPTER 5

WHY POWER MATTERS

PAUSING TO REFLECT ON WHERE YOU CAN FIND THE BEST possible outcome is the first step to getting what you want. But there's another factor that helps you to determine what possible options and outcomes could look like: power.

The thing about power is that it's unlike the other factors discussed previously. It's a little trickier. It's what fuels your negotiations. Having more power means having more options. And you want options. So, given its importance, what do you need to know about power? In this chapter, we'll discuss the two types of power and the benefits of being judicious in your use of it.

THERE IS ACTUAL POWER AND PERCEIVED POWER

Without power, you're at the mercy of the other party and there's little you can do but bend to their will. After all, what choice do you have if they have some type of leverage over you that they can use to force your hand? It's not a great situation to be in, and it makes it difficult to get what you want . . . but not impossible.

"*Whaaat*?!" Yup. You may not be as stuck as you think—because it's not just *actual* power that matters; *perceived* power counts as well. Having all the power in the world makes no difference if you don't use it (or if others don't even know you have it), and being powerless may not be so harmful if they have no clue that you don't have any power.

Say you're a manufacturer that is extremely dependent on our hypothetical retailer from the last chapter, GR, to whom you're selling 38 percent of your product. That's a huge chunk of your sales. If they take you off their shelves, it'll mean idle time in your factories, lost profits and layoffs. If you're producing less, you lose economies of scale, which means your product is more expensive to make and you'll have to raise your prices. Who knows what *that* would do to your remaining business.

In my example in chapter 4, the possibility that my client's product might be replaced unquestionably made them feel less powerful. The knowledge that if it *was* replaced, there would be some heavy consequences—perhaps even the loss of their jobs—stripped away more power. But the *last* thing the client needed to do was let on that they were as worried as they actually were, or the demands would just get bigger and tougher. Nor could they afford to bend to the will of the retailer; meeting its demands wasn't sustainable either.

What to do? First, they had to appear as if they had power (don't let them see you sweat). Then they had to figure out how to build up their actual power.

The client needed information, and they needed it quick. They needed to know if it was possible for the retailer to do what they were threatening to do. They did a study to find out the likelihood of GR being able to find the raw materials and having the factory capacity to make a similar product. The findings of the study were favorable to the client on both counts, thus building up their power—a double whammy! To gain even more power, the client also got data on brand loyalty to figure out whether consumers would buy a store-brand substitute. And then started a series of presentations with each of the retailer's stakeholders, a "road show" of sorts, to showcase that the manufacturer not only offered levels of innovation and service that everyone needed for a smooth shopping experience for the consumer, but they could also demonstrate such a high degree of consumer loyalty that shoppers would be looking for the product on the retailer's shelves—and if they didn't find it, would take their spending money elsewhere.

This was a game changer. As soon as my client showed the buyers that replacing the product with a store-brand alternative wasn't going to be so easy, it changed the nature of the discussion and led to a more efficient conversation. The manufacturer's objective was to close a deal that would save its existing business for at least another few years and not have to break the bank to do it. It managed to close a three-year deal and secure shelf space for *additional* products thanks to grace under pressure, supported by an effective strategy.

The client's strategy was to change the *perception* of power and build actual power in this negotiation. The retailer was acting as if it had all of the power and the supplier was its puppet (a common theme in this industry these days), and that wasn't doing my client any favors. When you have no power, you have no options. You have to give the other party whatever they demand. On the other hand, if you can increase your power, you increase your options.

A FULL BATTERY GIVES YOU MORE OPTIONS

When you charge your smartphone, you've got enough power to do whatever you want on it: watch videos, play games, chat with friends, use social media—even use the dial pad to speak to someone. But if your battery is low, you won't have the option to do all of those things. You'll have to minimize your activities. That might mean a less productive or less enjoyable experience. When you've got a full battery, you can choose to watch that YouTube video or FaceTime with your dog. When that low-battery warning message pops up, all of a sudden those options aren't available to you anymore. You may not have ever wanted to FaceTime with your dog, but as soon as the option is taken away from you, it creates a little pang of panic. You start scrambling to find a charger or an outlet somewhere because "WHAT IF FLUFFY MISSES ME?!"

That moment when the panic strikes is precisely when you need to hit that pause button again and realize that FaceTiming with a dog is ridiculous (yeah, I'm judging you now) and you don't have time to play that extra round of Candy Crush anyway. And, oh yeah, you have a spare battery in your backpack (or you're going to be home, where your charger is waiting for you, in a few minutes).

The more power you have, the easier it is to operate everywhere on the negotiation spectrum. If you've got a full battery, you can operate anywhere from the collaborative, light side of the spectrum all the way to the darkest side and do so credibly. But if you're running low, you won't make it all the way to the My Way side, and you'll have to find a way to get the other party to play nicely in the Our Way parts of the spectrum. In order to get the most out of a My Way scenario and persuade the other party to yield to your demands, you need to have significant power. If you're desperate and go into a dark negotiation demanding that someone increase their offer to you when they know they could get a better deal by going elsewhere or by waiting a little longer, you don't stand a chance of looking credible. Why would they part with their cash, something that's so valuable, if they don't have to?

YOU CAN DECIDE WHEN TO USE YOUR POWER (AND WHEN NOT TO)

Paradoxically, just because you *have* all the power in the negotiation doesn't mean you have to—or should—*use* all of it. Just like with your phone, you may want to save some power for later, or maybe you just don't need it right now. You're having a good time without your phone (gasp!) and Fluffy is busy at the dog park, so there's no need to use up power on a video call with her. You may even consider that if you use the phone now, you won't have it when something more important comes up later. If you drain the battery now, recharging it will take a while, so you want to be mindful of when and how much you use your phone. The same principle applies to negotiation. Can you imagine using your power on your spouse or partner every time you have the opportunity?

"We're going to eat what I want every night since I'm the only one who knows how to cook" wouldn't go over well for too long. There are likely better ways to resolve that negotiation.

Often, it's possible to get My Way results while operating in a lighter Our Way zone. You could actually find a way to make the other party feel like they're getting something out of it, too. If you're consistently exercising your power in a situation that has an ongoing relationship, it's likely you'll lose that relationship. The other party will start looking for different options as a way to build up their power. It may not happen immediately, but give them enough time to charge their battery and you'll see what can happen.

Of course, the flip side is that power is useful only when it's being used. Store that battery for too long and it can lose its charge. Sitting on power without the other party knowing you have it isn't going to change anything between you. Perception of power is just as important as actual power, and if the other party thinks you have none, they'll operate under that assumption even if you have loads of it.

In every negotiation, power is going to be a factor, whether you're consciously aware of it or not. It would be prudent to press pause to figure out how much power you have, how much power you'll need to get the best deal, and how to use your power to get the other party to come to the side of the spectrum that's going to work best for you. Of course, in order to do that, you need to know where power comes from. In the next few chapters, we'll explore what charges your negotiation battery (confidence, options, knowledge) and what drains it (anxiety, dependence, time pressure).

CHAPTER 6

ANXIETY DRAINS AND CONFIDENCE GAINS

WHEN I READ ALL OF THE TERM PAPERS FROM MY MBA students at the end of the semester, the word that comes up most frequently is *anxiety*. It's often cited as the reason why people sign up for my class in the first place. And it's *always* the most frequent subject of conversation whenever I'm approached by audience members at a speaking event. I usually hear something like "I always get so much anxiety when I'm faced with a negotiation." It's no surprise that when you're facing a potential conflict, it stirs up some emotions. And if you're someone who avoids conflict or confrontation, it's guaranteed to cause some anxiety.

Countless studies on emotions and performance suggest that fear and anxiety can lead to suboptimal results. One of my favorites is a 2013 study by Harvard professor Alison Wood Brooks, who caused some anxiety in her participants by asking them to sing the Journey song "Don't Stop Believin'" in front of the group. I personally don't understand how ripping out a classic at the top of your lungs would cause anyone concern, but apparently it did. The participants were told to say, "I am anxious," "I am excited" or nothing at all before belting out the tune. According to a computer that measured each singer's volume and pitch, the ones who described themselves as excited performed better than the other two groups. They also performed better in a math test and a speech test. In the speech test, they spoke longer and were perceived as more persuasive, confident and persistent. By putting their brains in an opportunity mindset instead of a threat mindset, they improved their cognitive abilities. If your math skills and your confidence are taking a dive, imagine what that means for your negotiation outcomes.

People experiencing anxiety are likely to make weaker offers and try to just finish the darn thing as quickly as possible—even if that means leaving money on the table—to relieve their anxiety. In a 2011 study Brooks did with Maurice Schweitzer, they found that anxious negotiators made deals that were 12 percent less financially attractive than those made by neutral negotiators (those who hadn't been listening to the frightening soundtrack from the horror film *Psycho*). According to Brooks, research shows that "feeling or looking anxious results in suboptimal negotiation outcomes." It undeniably shows the need to reframe your anxiety as excitement to achieve better results.

Other behavioral specialists recommend breathing exercises, since we typically hold our breath when stressed. Every Saturday morning I hear my Pilates instructor remind our class to breathe as she sees some blue faces when the exercise gets intense.

The point is, figure out a way to handle your anxious energy. Find your mental pause button so you can reframe your anxiety as excitement or find some other coping mechanism, or you'll be draining your battery and charging theirs. If the other party smells insecurity or fear, it charges their battery. Confidence, however, will do the opposite. If you go in as cool as a cucumber, you may take the wind out of their sails (to mix metaphors). Not only will you put forward better proposals, but the other party will not see you as someone they can easily manipulate. The perception of confidence is a key to your negotiation success.

It doesn't matter if you have all the power in the world. If the other party *thinks* you have none, then you're in trouble. If you don't know how to *use* it, you're in trouble. In the early 2010s, I was approached by a client who needed some help with a high-stakes negotiation. Nowadays, you can get a credit card to collect points you can redeem on almost anything: travel, cash back, merchandise and gift cards are all up for grabs. Starbucks points? You got it. Want to go to the movies more often? There's a card for that too. Want to use your points to pay down your cell phone bill? Some telecom companies have their own cards. But when this client came to me, there weren't nearly as many loyalty cards to choose from, and theirs were the most popular ones out there. My client's rewards card was their flagship product, and it was the best program on the market. One of the largest banks in Canada (let's call it ABC Bank) was the client's bank-issued credit card partner, and it had the exclusive rights to this program. Canadians were eager to sign up for a card that allowed them to earn my client's points, so that meant they took their business to ABC.

When it was nearing time for the partnership agreement with ABC to come up for renewal, the rewards folks were nervous. They told me that in eighteen months they were going to be up against some tough negotiators who had all of the power and that the future of their business, their ability to get their rewards points into the hands of consumers, was at risk. This was a problem I was excited to sink my teeth into. The client sent over a ton of PowerPoint decks and background information for me to go through. I pored over pages and pages of data and thought, "I must have missed something." I had been told that the bank had all of the power, but everything I was reading indicated that the opposite was true. My client had a program that anyone would have been dying to be associated with. If ABC lost this program, it would be really hard for the bank to find or build a similar program that would get consumers equally excited to sign up with them as opposed to going to another bank to sign up for a different rewards card. My client's reward program was the reason consumers were flocking to *this* bank and racking up all of those valuable interest charges.

I went back to the client and asked what I was missing. I conducted some research interviews and dug a little deeper, and it still wasn't totally making sense to me. I thought I must be misunderstanding some critical element, perhaps something about the industry I hadn't yet grasped. How on Earth did the bank have so much power in this situation? Then we did a training program as part of the client's preparation for the negotiation. That's when it struck *everyone*. To the bank, the way my clients were handling their interactions with their counterparts at ABC just screamed insecurity and desperation. After all, if you behave like you desperately need me, I'm going to believe it and I'm going to hold it over your head.

After a few days locked up in a hotel conference room together, we had undone some of the bad habits the rewards people had been exhibiting with the bank, and things started to change.

Their mannerisms and language shifted. The language and timing of their emails no longer screamed of desperation and the need to please, and they stopped automatically agreeing to every tiny demand. (The Communication section of this book is full of specific examples of what *not* to do.) The entire executive team that had gone through the training program (those who were intimately involved in the high-level negotiations) began to have aha moments and recognized why they were being treated as if they were powerless.

When someone videotapes you in a negotiation simulation and plays it back for you, breaking it down in a play-by-play so that you hear every "um" and see every nervous tic, it's hard to deny. After all, a picture is worth a thousand words. The bank perceived my client as powerless because my client had been acting that way forever! When the bank said, "Jump," the team replied, "How high?" This dynamic had been going on for years, so we needed to enact some changes before the heavy-duty contract negotiations got underway. We put together an action plan to adjust the power dynamic and started working on what to say and do in those day-to-day meetings that would start to change the game. By the time the contract negotiations began, over a year later, the power dynamics had shifted and a whole new set of opportunities had opened themselves up to my clients. It all started with having the confidence and self-control to show up like you deserve to be there.

Until you act like you deserve to be treated with respect, it's going to be hard to get it, especially from someone who feels as though they have power over you. As I've said, this lack of confidence and self-control is something that is a massive challenge for so many of the people I encounter in my work. It's become a focal point for so much of my professional speaking career and a massive focus of every training and development workshop I run for corporate clients. Rita, one of my most experienced MBA students, shared a noteworthy observation about her insecurity and discomfort with negotiation:

> *Immediately after the first class in the course I asked myself the question: "On a scale of one to ten, where ten stands for 'you have every confidence that you are an effective negotiator' and one stands for the opposite, what number would you give yourself?" In that first class, I rated my confidence as an effective negotiator as a four out of ten. But by class number 11, twelve weeks later, I rated my confidence as seven out of ten. I then asked myself: "What got me from four to seven?"*
>
> *The answer was practice.*

Funnily enough, I actually ask my clients to use a similar rating system before they start an intensive training program with me, followed by the same question at the end of the session. The average rating goes from a 6 to an 8.7. Given all of the research about the effects of reducing anxiety, this gives me reason to believe that those clients are going to achieve much better results. Fortunately, they also provide me with data and anecdotes weeks and months later that prove that our time together means better profitability—real-life examples of what some attitudinal changes and a few little tips and tricks can do.

Going back to the example of the manufacturer, if my clients had gone into negotiations with the retailer reeking of fear and insecurity, not only would they have made weaker offers (dooming themselves from the beginning), but it also would have been a signal for the retailer to go for the jugular and extract everything it could. The road show I mentioned was an opportunity for my clients to puff out their chests, demonstrate their value and show their confidence in what they brought to the table (innovation, quality, consumer loyalty, etc.). The goal was to signal to the other party that the battery was charging and that they were a worthy partner instead of a weak adversary.

How do you beat anxiety? Practice. Before going into every one of those "shows" or meetings, like my students, these folks had practiced. They had rehearsed their presentations and, more importantly, they had prepared for every question or statement we could possibly think of. That practice gave them the confidence to handle everything that came their way and show the other party that they deserved respect. They deserved to be approached with an Our Way mentality.

The ability to press that pause button and exercise the self-control required to not become a bumbling fool can lead to a sea change in the way the other party perceives you. And perception becomes reality in their mind. Give them a dose of reality that's going to work to your benefit. Use your pause button to calm your brain and redirect your energy into excitement instead of anxiety and find some ways to bring down that heart rate with meditative breaths—whatever it takes!

CHAPTER 7

DEPENDENCY DESPAIR AND BATNA POWER PLAYS

CONFIDENCE CAN'T BE THE ONLY FACTOR THAT DETER-
mines power in a negotiation. You can't just go in and puff out your
chest and shout, "I'm confident now, so do whatever I say!" There
needs to be some credibility to go along with it.

One vital factor that affects that credibility in the power equation is the dependency you have on each other. If you are fully
dependent on the other party—if you need them and have no other
option—you're going to be powerless. If, for example, you want to
renovate your historic house while keeping the original style intact,
you'll have to find someone who has experience with restoration
projects. Odds are, those craftsmen are few and far between. When
you finally manage to track down that person who has the unique
skill set you're looking for and happens to be available when you
need them, you'll find yourself in a challenging negotiation. If that
person is the only one in town who can perfectly preserve those
staircase spindles, then it will be tough to negotiate them away from
the rate they quote you. If they *know* they're the only one around
with experience, and that if you don't get those stairs repaired,

you're going to be in trouble—perhaps even have a safety issue on your hands—your dependency on them increases further. That's power they now have over you.

If, however, you decide you don't care about historic preservation—you just want something functional, maybe even a little more modern—that opens up a whole new set of options. There are likely a lot more carpenters who can rebuild a set of stairs if you're not so picky about what they look like, especially if you're cool with the standard spindles available at every big-box store. With a lengthy list of carpenters to choose from, all of a sudden you've got power. You can tell this preservation specialist to take a hike because you can hire one of the other twenty-five options you found in your Google search. If you can easily swap out one contractor for another, that gives *you* leverage or power in this negotiation. The less dependent you are on the other party, the more power you have.

This list of other carpenters is referred to as a BATNA in negotiation theory. It's a term coined by Harvard professors Roger Fisher and William Ury in their 1981 bestseller *Getting to Yes* (the granddaddy of all negotiation books), and it stands for the **B**est **A**lternative **T**o a **N**egotiated **A**greement. The idea is that if a negotiation falls apart, you consider your next best option—your plan B. And if you've got several other options that are nearly as good as your first choice, you're sitting pretty.

Obviously, the negotiation you're getting into should be happening for a reason; otherwise, it's a waste of your energy. Where plan A is concerned, the other party must offer something the alternatives don't. In this example, maybe that something extra is that the carpenter you want to hire comes highly recommended, while the ones in your Google search are strangers, so your primary option carries less risk. Maybe it's that they're willing to do the work faster or on your schedule, so you don't have to rearrange your appointments. If you can get the carpenter you want at a price you're willing to pay, you're all set. *But,* if that primary negotiation doesn't work out and you're not devastated, it's because you've got a decent plan B. If you've also got plans C through Z, you've got a good amount of power going into this negotiation. The more BATNAs you have, the more power you have. (Just remember that your BATNA has to be somewhat desirable, so if it sends shivers down your spine or will land you in jail, don't get too cocky, my friends.)

Going back to my loyalty program client, if ABC Bank had plenty of other programs it could swap in—programs that would attract nearly as many new credit card holders as the original one—it would have as much power as the rewards company thought it did. But if ABC's BATNA had been a program that wasn't appealing enough to consumers to lure them in and sign up for the credit card, that alternative wasn't going to do it any favors. For example, what if the bank started advertising, "We've got a new credit card that lets you accumulate points to redeem on your favorite cigarettes"? In the US and Canada, less than 20 percent of the population smokes, so the bank would only be marketing to a small fraction of the population—plus, I'm not sure how many consumers would be proud to whip out that credit card, given the social stigma attached to smoking. Such a weak BATNA would mean terrible results for the bank (maybe even a public relations nightmare), which would make it a lot more dependent on the original loyalty program provider.

So, we've seen that the stronger the BATNA, the more power you have. Quality and quantity of BATNAs both contribute to power. Conversely, being able to weaken the other party's BATNA is a way to increase their dependency on you. If, as a homeowner, you know a thing or two about historic houses and are aware that the trend is toward modern-style renovations, you may be able to squash the specialist carpenter's BATNA. You can point out that if they think they're going to have a mass of customers calling for quotes, they're in for a rude awakening. The idea that they *need* this project to fill their time and pay the bills may make the carpenter feel weak enough that they back off of their high price point.

At the rewards group, we had plenty of data to show that customers would follow the program to a new bank—and a new card—if the partnership with ABC was severed (this was why I was so confused about who had the power in my initial assessment). That's a compelling argument to make ABC back off of its My Way approach to negotiations and start working a little closer to Our Way. They were made more aware of their dependency (and of the fact we knew how dependent they were), making it difficult to operate at the dark, My Way side of the spectrum.

Remember, when we operate on the dark side of the spectrum, it's typically because of leverage that we can use without worrying about the other party walking away. If you don't have significant power (actual and/or perceived) and you try to operate in that price-focused My Way dimension, it will be hard to do so credibly. And if you don't have credibility, the strategy will likely backfire. The other party will only feel *more* powerful if they think you look foolish. They could even laugh in your face.

If you *do* have BATNAs that give you power, but the other party has no idea and thus still perceives you as weak, it's going to be a tough road—just as tough as if you were to go in with no confidence. So, you may want to drop some hints about theirs not being your only option, or about them not being the only game in town. You'll see an example of this in the next section.

Developing some BATNAs before you go into any negotiation or finding some way to squash the other party's BATNAs is a good way to increase your confidence and your power in the negotiation. You'll feel much better and you'll get better results; even if you don't want to use those BATNAs, you know you've charged your battery. Knowing you aren't so dependent on the other party, and helping them see that they are dependent on you, will also help you drain their battery and charge your own, helping you create options no matter where you want to operate on the spectrum. You can go from begging them to work with Our Way to imposing My Way on them, if that's what your needs require.

CHAPTER 8

THE TIME PRESSURE IS ON

TIME PRESSURE CAN DRAMATICALLY AFFECT POWER IN A negotiation. As we've discussed, the amount of time a negotiation takes can change the style of the discussion (shorter-term talks occupy the dark/My Way side of the spectrum, while longer-term ones take place more on the light/Our Way end), but how does that translate into power? Remember that negotiations on the darker side are the least complex, focusing primarily on cost, which makes them colder and cagier. When you have power, you can operate this way if you want to, but you don't have to if you can see a better option on the more creative, complex side. Meanwhile, when you don't have much power, it's going to be tough to pressure the other party to speed up and meet your demands.

If one of the parties is pressed for time, it can also dramatically affect the balance of power in negotiations. If you're in a rush to conclude negotiations because you have a deadline to meet, that's definitely going to affect your power. That deadline adds pressure, and we already know what pressure can do to our brains: irrational things. If there's a way for you to press pause to reduce the urgency, that will help prevent your battery from getting drained.

Imagine you're at a car dealership, telling the dealer that your current car is breaking down and you need a new one today so you don't get stuck by the side of the road on your way to work tomorrow. It's going to be hard to credibly convince them to bring down their price if they know they're your only option and you need what they've got *right now*. They're going to feel smug and resist lowering the price much, if any. If you tell them you can easily go down the street to the next car dealer (your BATNA), that can drain their battery a little and recharge yours. But if time is of the essence, it's going to be tough to keep that battery from draining, especially if the dealer knows you don't have time to run around. That knowledge empowers them to make you pay the highest possible price for the car.

When you're under time pressure, it's easy for irrational thoughts to crowd out the rational thought process and make you forget you have the ability to apply some pressure on the dealer as well. Instead of disclosing that you're under the gun to buy a new car, what if you were to tell the dealer, "You've got ten minutes before I head to the next dealership on my list," or "I've got an appointment with another dealer in an hour"? Now you've turned the tables, transferring a bit of the pressure to the other party. This keeps you from letting your battery run down, while causing them to drain theirs to some degree.

This is why you often see folks assigning deadlines or expiration times to their offers. "This is a limited-time offer" and "This price is good for today only" are common sales tactics. But buyers will do the same thing. If you've ever been involved in a real estate trans-action, you may have come across buyers who placed time limits on their offers—for example, declaring that an offer was only good until 5 p.m. on the day it was made. Those arbitrary deadlines are designed to cue the fight-or-flight instinct in your brain that sends all rational thought out the window. It's the reason we need that darn pause button I talked about earlier.

When faced with a deadline, pause to ask yourself, "Is this a legitimate deadline or a fabricated one?" It's not as though a bomb is about to explode and you need to hightail it out of there before a 007-type explosion occurs. A negotiation is simply two (or more) people having a conversation. So, talk about what is driving this time limit and try to find out whether it's merely a negotiation tac-tic or if something else is happening—perhaps the opportunity will disappear because another buyer is coming in, or because the other party is under pressure to move on to another deal.

Years ago, when I worked in manufacturing and dealt on a reg-ular basis with the corporate teams at global retailers, I was often told, "I need you to get back to me by end of day." I would pause and think, "What difference is it going to make if I get back to you by the end of the day, when you're getting ready to leave or are already gone for the day?" It's not as though they would run back to the office and deal with my answer right then and there.

In my years of working in that industry, I dealt with only one true deadline. One of my favorite buyers (who never set artificial deadlines) offered me a last-minute opportunity to advertise May-belline mascara in her flyer. The flyer was going to be printed that day. We needed to get the official paperwork and artwork from my marketing department before 5 p.m. or her company wouldn't be able to include it. I scrambled like crazy and called in favors from all over the place to make it happen because it was important to me, and I could tell it was a legitimate deadline for the flyer production team. But when other "deadlines" were given, I would politely tell my counterparts I understood that they were feeling some pressure and I would get back to them as soon as I was able, whatever that meant. People were generally responsive and appreciative of my acknowledging them, and the deadlines magically disappeared. Most of the time, there was some trust between us, which made some of those icky tactics dissipate.

One of my students, Dominica, told me about a recent negotiation that she encountered where she had the opportunity to use time to increase her power:

> I negotiated a deal with a student who was subleasing a room. I paused and realized that besides the rent, this negotiation also involved a number of other factors, such as the move-in date, housekeeping, utilities and maintenance. I'd also done my research and calculated the average rent that other students in the building were paying. During my investigation, I realized that the reason the [student] wanted to rent out the room was that she had to attend to an important task back home and did not want to leave the place vacant. This proved beneficial for me, as I had the power of time on my side.
>
> The negotiation was carried out via Facebook chat, which gave me the opportunity to pause and think logically

before replying to each of her offers. I made counteroffers covering multiple issues, including the fact that I was willing to move in early and take on the lease for the entire period that she would be away. I finally signed off on a deal with a rent amount that was lower than the average rent in the building, along with the cost of utilities covered instead of paying them out of my pocket.

Knowing that the landlord was in a rush to leave and make sure that the room wasn't left empty for long gave Dominica the leverage she needed to lower her rent and utility costs. Ultimately, the landlord paid for that time pressure.

If you were to meet Dominica, you'd know that she is not aggressive. She is extremely polite and respectful, and I have no doubt that's exactly how she handled this discussion. Negotiation doesn't have to be rude or nasty for you to get what you want. If you press pause to consider the situation and the pressures the other party may be experiencing, you can increase your power, making it a little easier to get your way without having to get aggressive.

Now, if Dominica were feeling equal time pressure to get into a place quickly, she might have handled things differently (though I hope she would have been just as calm and cool). This raises an interesting question: if both parties are under pressure to get a deal done by the first of the month, which side should be exerting the time pressure? The answer is: the one who can do so most credibly, and that's inevitably the one with the most power (actual and/or perceived). Which side has the better BATNAs and the most confidence? Confidence often starts out strong on both sides, but as the deadline approaches and the end of the conversation nears, that's when the fight-or-flight impulse kicks into high gear and irrational thought takes over. Mistakes are made and batteries are drained. If you can press the pause button and maintain your composure, you're more likely to obtain bigger and more rapid concessions.

I do simulations in my MBA classes and client workshops. Students and clients are given situations for negotiation with a deadline, and inevitably the talks start out quite calm and cool on both sides. Eventually, no matter how long I give them—it could be five minutes or it could be forty-five—as soon as they realize they have only 20 percent of their time remaining, they start to feel the time pressure and there's a mad dash to make concessions. In the five-minute negotiations I have clients conduct on video, I give them a quiet one-minute warning, and you can see the moment when the panic sets in. All of a sudden there's a lot more talking, louder talking, and more animated body language. It's actually quite comical. The person who manages to keep their cool in that moment is always the one who gets a better deal.

Pressure is exerted to encourage concessions in order to reach agreement more efficiently. Studies show us time and again that negotiators under time pressure in a competitive negotiation start making more frequent concessions, so the longer you pause, the more pressure they feel. Sometimes they start negotiating against themselves, so you don't even need to make a counteroffer. They just keep throwing out offers and becoming more agreeable until you say yes. They also increase the *size* of the concessions in an attempt to close the deal. Those giant moves signal desperation, a drained battery and a bending to the other party's power and will.

If the other party's ego trumps their drained battery (the ultimate in irrational thought), then even being powerless won't get them to agree. There are just some negotiators who would rather harm themselves than see you win. It's safe to assume you'd be the one with the power in this situation and thus can move on to your BATNA, since that's where some of that power came from anyway.

As I was writing this chapter, a neighbor at the office was telling me about his timely (no pun intended) negotiation. He's in the process of selling his business. The negotiations have been going on for some time, and he has been somewhat frustrated at the lack of progress on getting a complete offer from the prospective buyer, who is still working on raising funds from investors. The buyer keeps insisting they can start the transition by having a gentlemen's agreement and "work out the details later." Ugh. If you're nearing the end of a negotiation and you still don't have the final details, that means the clock is working against you.

In psychological speak, this tendency to be consistent with our previous actions, even when doing so is against our own interests, is called a commitment bias. In economics, it's known as the sunk cost fallacy—since I've already dropped so much time, money, energy, etc., into this effort, I'll just make an irrational decision to see it through. It's the same reasoning you would use at a losing slot machine in Las Vegas—you figure that because you've already invested this much, you might as well stick around because the machine is bound to pay out.

As time passes in any negotiation, your subconscious is freaking out, convincing you not to let all of this time and energy go to waste. Remember, though: the house always wins. And this situation is no different. So, my neighbor is rightfully holding off on any agreements, gentlemen's or otherwise, until there is a satisfactory offer on the table. We'll have a lot more to discuss about how biases affect negotiation in section 3.

When someone is asking you to "work out the details later," this should be a big warning that time is being used against you to drain your power. Work out the details while you still have power and leverage. Once you're already in the execution phase of the agreement, the clock will be spinning forward and you'll be the one facing some serious time pressure, impeding your ability to get your way.

On the My Way side of the spectrum, artificial time pressures are often applied as a way to exploit the power differential between the parties, and it's usually the party with more power who is trying to speed up the process and exploit the side with less power, causing them to lower their demands. When used in Our Way situations, time pressures can hinder creativity and problem solving—which are the cornerstones of this type of negotiation.

Harvard's Dr. Teresa Amabile found that the more workers feel crunched for time, the less likely they are to solve tricky problems. She theorizes that time pressure crushes creativity because it limits the freedom to consider different options and possibilities. In a 2002 talk she gave to the American Psychological Association, she said, "Think of it as the way you may enter a maze and explore for a solution. With increased time pressure, you take the simplest pathway, not one that's elegant or creative. But if you're able to spend more time exploring the maze, you're more likely to hit on exciting new solutions."

Her research found that employees were 45 percent less likely to think creatively on high-pressure days than they were on low-pressure days. The only exception occurred when employees were allowed to focus undisturbed on a single activity deemed truly important. Negotiations rarely include solo reflection time, but if you can find a way to build in that kind of time, maybe you can spur some creative solutions.

The lighter side of the negotiation spectrum requires creativity and problem-solving skills to deal with complex situations. Waiting until the last minute, or imposing time pressure, limits solutions and forces us to the dark side of the spectrum to focus on a quick solution, narrowing the focus down to money alone. That can be costly. Furthermore, searching for creative solutions on those high-pressure days is not going to produce much inspired thought, so you may want to start early or spread out the process.

ANTICIPATING DEADLINES

My manufacturer friends are a great example of how timelines can be managed to facilitate productive conversation and protect against being manipulated by combative retailers exerting time pressure. The first thing to do is map out a timeline of when the manufacturer thinks it will be under the most time pressure and start blocking out time in calendars and coordinating more productive discussions with its counterparts at Global Retailer. My clients reach out with meeting requests weeks apart, with the sole purpose of making sure they are guaranteed some face-to-face contact with their counterparts. This ensures that they don't get caught up in a rush to make an agreement without the appropriate amount of time for internal discussions and brainstorming. The rewards company went as far as planning a series of regular meetings with its banking counterparts months before the contract deadline so that they could do the same. By making sure they were in charge of time and were influencing the process early, they were able to minimize the likelihood of the other party using time pressures to steer the negotiation into the competitive, My Way side of the spectrum. It was a way to keep their batteries charged and prevent the other side from being able to drain them.

Time pressures foster a short-term mentality that can benefit you if you're operating on the dark, My Way side of the spectrum. But remember that triggering this source of stress for the other party can cause efficient and collaborative, value-focused solutions to be overlooked. Knowing a deadline far in advance can help both parties plan appropriately to ensure that they have enough time to work through complex scenarios and come up with an Our Way solution. Competitive negotiators who favor the My Way approach are unlikely to use deadlines for that purpose, so be wary of who it is that you're dealing with and anticipate those deadlines to make sure you're not stuck in a battery-draining time crunch. Being able to anticipate how long a negotiation will take, along with preparing for any potential deadlines, will help you build up your confidence, which will charge your battery.

PAUSING AS A TACTIC

Being able to pause for even a few seconds can change the way you interact with others and increase the success of your negotiation outcomes. Take this story that one of my MBA students recently shared with me:

> *My disagreements with my spouse don't escalate as quickly as they used to, especially because I take the time to listen to her a lot more actively, and whenever I feel like I may give a response that would not be well received by her, I take a pause to help me choose my words in a way that doesn't worsen the situation. Taking a pause helps me compose my thoughts and hold off from reacting.*
>
> *For example, last weekend, I was studying for one of my exams and my spouse asked me to get some pasta sauce. My general response, especially when I am under the stress of an exam, would have been, "I am busy studying for my exam tomorrow and cannot get it right now." Pressing the pause prevented me from making the assumption that she wants me to go to the grocery store right away. My response was, "Would it be okay if I get this after half an hour, after I finish this chapter?" and it helped satisfy interests of both of us.*

Taking a pause to create suspense is another way of using time to your advantage, draining the other side's battery in a way that yields some positive side effects for you, as this student shared:

> *Previously, it felt like pausing was a sign of weakness where someone could take advantage of me if they perceived that I didn't know what to say. In fact, the exact opposite was*

true. This pause allowed me to maintain my composure and prevent emotions from taking over. My perception of power was not impacted; if anything, it built more suspense and emphasis as my counterpart eagerly waited for my response.

And sometimes it can help in situations where you're trying to negotiate for people's attention and agreement, as another student recalled:

I have tried to incorporate pauses during my presentations, and I feel a lot more confident in my presentation abilities. I noticed that the pauses help me connect with the audience better, as well as give me the opportunity to breathe and relax every now and then . . . to help me maintain my composure when I am in front of an audience. Even though I am far from being a rock star on stage, taking deep breaths and power poses before beginning my presentation and consciously introducing pauses during my presentation to [emphasize] an important point have made me more comfortable in front of an audience and has also made my delivery more effective.

Pausing may seem counterintuitive. I mean, why would I slow down when I'm feeling pressure to get things done faster? But we slow down to speed up. Creating a few seconds of clarity and rational thought can prevent minutes or hours (or longer) of combative behavior and perhaps even resentment for a long time to come. The ability to manage time and get ahead of it is what will help you keep your battery charged and potentially help you drain the other party's, if that's your goal.

CHAPTER 9

THE MORE YOU KNOW

"KNOWLEDGE IS POWER" IS A PHRASE MOST OF US KNOW and can get behind. And it is clearly valid in the world of negotiation. When you do your research before a negotiation, you are charging your battery. Take some time to consider the person you are dealing with before the negotiation takes place: Do they have a pattern of behavior that can help you plan your negotiation strategy? If you're on a beach in Punta Cana, watching other tourists negotiate with vendors for parasailing excursions, and you've observed that some vendors are going as low as $40 for a ride after a few counterproposals with the guests, then you know better than to fall for the guy asking for a hundred bucks who insists he's offering the lowest price. You'll know enough to make a much lower counteroffer and get the market rate (or better).

At home, if you know your child always fakes a stomachache when the vegetables are put on her plate, you know to ask how she's feeling before you plate the dish, thus erasing at least one of her excuses for the time being.

In the corporate world, observing patterns has been extremely helpful for so many of my clients. People can be predictable creatures, especially when they're spread thin, trying to manage a ton of negotiations at once. One global retailer, which shall remain nameless, had a team that was notorious for making a ridiculously extreme demand for cash every year. They were also notorious for cutting that demand in half within weeks of the initial ultimatum. One of my clients was so consumed with the pressure the crazy demand created that they didn't even notice the pattern until I came in and started asking about the series of proposals over the past two years. Being able to see the pattern relieved a lot of pressure and allowed them to create an effective strategy. In my work with another client, we realized that the person in charge of negotiations for the other party asked, "Is that your best offer?" at the end of every negotiation. This question usually resulted in my client feeling extra pressure and scrambling to throw something else on the table. Once we dug into the history and spotted that pattern, we found ways to prevent it and eliminate the scrambling. (More on that negotiation later in the Process section.)

In a salary negotiation, knowing the market trends and gathering information about average salaries within the organization or industry will help you go in not only with some confidence (power), but also with some objective, undisputable justifications for your expectations instead of the school of personal opinion. Knowing what qualities and skills decision makers are expecting for a given role will help you frame what you bring to the table while encountering less resistance. Knowing which elements of the compensation package have been negotiable in the past gives you a road map to where you can find some easy wins. Understanding even more about creative compensation opportunities can help you find even more unconventional ways to increase your total pay package.

Understanding who the decision makers actually are in any negotiation—and who influences them—can help you build rapport with the folks who are going to have a hand in affecting the outcome. Recalling something about their personal life that they have shared with you (not something you discovered in a creepy, stalker-ish way) can go a long way toward building that rapport and trust with key players. You may also want to know a little about their personal preferences and patterns. When I worked in a food manufacturing company, I knew that my buyers were early risers and left the office by 4:30 p.m. at the latest. I also knew that time of day was a major factor in how agreeable they were. Dawn was when they would be in the best mood—and the least distracted putting out everyday fires—compared to the end of the day. I recall getting hold of one of them at 4 p.m. and asking if she was free to talk about an initiative we were working on together. Her answer? "You've got my attention until my car pool shows up, and then I'm outta here." Talk about time pressure. I switched to early-morning calls and started drinking a lot of coffee for the first time in my life. It might have been rough for this not-so-early riser, but it made my negotiations a lot easier.

From a more strategic standpoint, understanding what is driving or motivating the negotiator to talk to you is a powerful nugget of information you can use to your advantage. Remember, they wouldn't be giving you the time of day if they didn't have some need for this negotiation. If you're at the car dealership, it's helpful to know whether they're struggling to make a quota at the end of the month—or quarter, or year. Consider what pressures they might be facing that you could help them relieve if they were to help you in return. What keeps them up at night that you could take care of? How useful would you be to them? There's that dependency that we talked about earlier.

As you can see, knowing your counterparts and their patterns is extremely valuable. If you're dealing with someone who has a different cultural background, then be aware of some of their cultural practices as well. You don't want to inadvertently offend them and start the negotiation off on the wrong foot. Be careful of making assumptions about their cultural norms, however. I have the privilege of teaching audiences and MBA students from all over the world. My students at York University, in Toronto, are a multicultural group. Some of them bring the competitive practices from the markets in their home countries into their negotiations, while others quickly adapt to the norms of their surroundings. Know the person and the circumstances to try to incorporate their behavior into your negotiation plan.

HOW DO YOU GET KNOWLEDGE?

There are four ways to gain that valuable knowledge that will charge your battery: doing research (observing patterns, using search engines), asking questions, using silence and sharing something about yourself.

To research your counterparts and their circumstances, pay attention to their social media posts, résumé changes and patterns of behavior in your interactions. I'm not suggesting stalking them, but pay attention to the information that is out there for you. This step is so often neglected and underestimated. It could be that a bit of Googling will provide you with enough information to set yourself up for success. Do be mindful of the credibility of your resources, though. Wikipedia can be edited by anyone, so it's not exactly reliable (that's why many academic institutions have banned it as a primary source). And if you're negotiating compensation, make sure to check that salary data websites are up to date and relevant to your market.

The second way to gain knowledge is to ask questions—people can be your greatest resources. Start asking people in your industry, network or inner circle for some wisdom and advice. Don't know anyone with relevant info? Ask your network who they might know. Speaking of people, the people sitting across from you in the negotiation are a resource you need to be prepared to mine for data. Be prepared to ask questions during the negotiation. (We'll talk about this a lot more in the Communication section.) Remember, when people are uncomfortable (and most people *are* uncomfortable in negotiations), their rational thought disappears and they often give themselves away. Resist the temptation to be the person giving things away, and instead ask the questions to get your counterparts to do all the talking. Of course, make sure you stay within moral (and legal) boundaries. You don't want to get caught up in collusion or other unsavory behaviors.

That brings me to the third method: silence. Take a pause. If you're too busy talking—and giving away information—the other party will never have enough "airtime" to give you that valuable stuff. Most of my students used to worry that if they were too quiet, they would be perceived as stupid or weak. I reassure them that it's important to pause to buy yourself time to think and consider the next words that are going to come out of your mouth. People are often so uncomfortable with silence that they feel the need to fill it with rambling, and that's a surefire way to drain your battery. As a consolation prize, I advise them to use questions (even questions they already know the answers to) to buy themselves time and potentially get some additional information from their counterparts.

The last technique I'll mention here is a bit counterintuitive: share something yourself. If you're both sitting there in silence because you don't trust each other enough to open up, then something's got to give. You can start the ball rolling by sharing some information and building a little bit of trust. Effective negotiators are mindful and measured in what they share, taking care not to reveal anything damaging (like how much money you have in your pocket), but sharing something that will help both parties to reveal preferences and show where they should be using their energy to craft better value. Fortunately, our subconscious minds go back to those tribal instincts where we want to mirror those around us, so if you share something, the other party is likely to start sharing information in return—potentially more than *you* provided—so long as you give them the airtime to do it.

Consider that the more you know, the more you can charge your battery and plan appropriately, no matter where you are on the spectrum. As you start to uncover ways that the other party could be dependent on you, what BATNAs are available to both parties, and what kind of time pressures may exist, you'll find ways to charge your battery and potentially drain theirs. I guess the NBC television network was on to something when they launched those "The More You Know" public service announcements a couple of decades ago.

Ultimately, knowledge will give you the confidence I talked about at the beginning of this section. The ability to pause and access all of this stuff that's in your brain will give you the bravado you need to walk in there like you own the joint. And the ability to consider the information that's in your counterpart's brain can make all the difference.

One of my favorite examples of the importance of knowledge and the confidence it brings comes from one of my students. Sasha worried that if she pushed for more, the other party might walk away from the negotiating table, leaving her with nothing—fear of the other side walking away is a huge source of anxiety for many negotiators. She went on to recall something I share with students and audiences all the time: There is a reason why the other party is sitting down at the table with you. If they didn't need you, they wouldn't be there. It was just as true in my manufacturer example. Those buyers at the global retailer have a zillion meetings a day. They won't give someone the time of day if they don't see the potential for that person to help them fulfill a need.

Sasha told me an uplifting story about a job offer negotiation she experienced after our class. She was called for an interview, and it went so well that they made her an offer:

I learned it is important to identify [the reason they are sitting down at the table with you] and play up my power in order to create the best integrative solution . . . I bring power, skills or products that the other party finds valuable and desirable, or they would not be speaking with me at all . . . Less than a week later, their human resources department called me to offer me the position. During that phone call I negotiated my salary, as I wanted to be on the other side of the statistic that we discussed in class that only 7 percent of women negotiate their job offers . . . I told them that based on the skill set I am bringing to their team, my experience, the fact that I will have my master's in disaster and emergency management . . . I was hoping there would be room to move on the salary to improve my job satisfaction. They told me that they would have to check with the budgeting department and my boss and get back to me. I felt very anxious that I would not hear back from them and that I had messed up my chances of landing this amazing job.

I had to keep reminding myself of my power throughout this waiting period. There was a reason they were offering me this job and having this conversation with me instead of with someone else. I had to remember my BATNA of two other potential opportunities in my field: keeping my current job, and [continuing] to take classes next semester instead of working full time.

With such strong BATNAs, if this job did not work out, I had multiple other satisfactory options. I would absolutely never have done something like this if I had not taken this negotiation class.

Two days after this phone negotiation, the human resources representative called me back and offered me a 5 percent increase from their original offer. He told me that he had to go back and forth with their budgeting department, as the budget was pre-established, to push for this increase for me . . . and that he really hoped I would choose to move forward with them and join their team. I, of course, wanted this job and would have accepted it at the original salary offered, and I accepted. I know that I will be much more satisfied knowing that I negotiated the offer instead of just accepting the original offer . . . It was really helpful applying what I learned in class to be able to recognize and play up my power in order to negotiate the salary for this job.

Sasha's ability to pause and focus on the knowledge that *they* needed *her* was the factor that gave her the confidence to move forward and get the 5 percent increase. It didn't hurt that she also considered the BATNAs and other factors that bolstered her position. With that power in hand, she was equipped to carry herself to a new level of job satisfaction.

PAUSE FOR REFLECTION

SECTION 2 | POWER ISN'T ALWAYS OBVIOUS
CHECKLIST OF KEY TAKEAWAYS

✓ **There are two types of power.** Actual and perceived power both affect your negotiation outcomes.

✓ **Power fuels your negotiation and provides options.** The more power you have, the more options you have to operate credibly. With less power, you'll be limited to the more collaborative side of the negotiation spectrum.

✓ **Power is not permanent.** You can charge or drain your battery; so, even when you have all the power, you need to choose when to use it and when to save some for later.

✓ **Anxiety drains your power.** Calming your anxiety with practice and other coping mechanisms will build your confidence and increase both your power and the odds of getting a great deal. You'll get them to back down or keep them from getting aggressive.

✓ **BATNAs are vital.** Developing some BATNAs before you go into any negotiation or finding some way to squash theirs is a good way to increase your confidence and charge your battery.

- ✓ **Managing time pressure is critical.** Getting sucked into feeling time pressure will trigger your fight-or-flight response and the irrational thoughts that come with it. Pressing your pause button and using time pressure to your advantage is extremely powerful.
- ✓ **Knowledge helps to create confidence.** It's a blueprint on where to find quick wins and prevent problems. Knowledge about the people you're dealing with and what is driving them gives you a road map to build solutions.
- ✓ **Get more power by acquiring knowledge.** Do some research, talk to people, practice being silent, and share a little something to get some information in return.
- ✓ **Why are you here?** Remember that there's a reason why people are negotiating with you in the first place. That's powerful stuff!

SECTION 3

PEOPLE OVER SPREADSHEETS

CHAPTER 10

THE X FACTOR OF NEGOTIATION

WHEN I THINK OF SOME OF THE MOST DIFFICULT, POWER-less negotiations I've faced, whether my own or those of clients, the factor that has helped to get us over the finish line has been people. We could consider relationships as another power factor, but they're so much more. They can override the power balance and prevent others from even wanting to exploit you. When you're stalled or hit a rough patch and the other party is trying to exploit that drained battery on the My Way side of the spectrum, your relationship with them can be the factor that helps you move them a tiny bit closer to Our Way. If you're aiming to keep the transaction 100 percent price-focused, and you know the people with whom you are exchanging that cash, people could also become your weakness. That human component can be a game changer.

I'd like to think that back in my manufacturing days, dealing with retail buyers, I had good relationships with all of the folks with whom I interacted. They told me as much, even after I quit the business. I even had a few buyers tell me, "I wish all of my vendors were as prepared as you," which I took as a massive compliment.

I don't share this to boast; it was an insight I took as a sign that they liked working with me, and I maintained my way of working when I moved into consulting. My relationships with my clients are the reason I ended up being self-employed—they asked me to keep working with them long after I quit my job at a consulting firm. They're the ones who told me, "We didn't hire the company, we hired you." If it weren't for these relationships, I don't think I ever would have started my own business.

RELATIONSHIPS HELP OVERRIDE RIGID PROCESSES

When I was a vendor selling to a giant retailer, it was my responsibility to meet with the buyers regularly to get them to keep buying my company's products and keep them stocked for consumers to purchase. You'd be shocked at how challenging that can be at times, but overall, it was a routine my team and I had down. One day, however, we received a forty-page document from a third party that outlined an auction process to keep our baking product on the shelves. The retailer had limited space and didn't need a lot of variety, so they were going to trim the product selection. Instead of seeing three or four brands of the same type of product, shoppers would find only two brands (one of which was likely to be the retailer's own brand). The buyers figured that with all of the extra room they would be creating on the shelf, they'd have greater quantities of the selected products, so consumers wouldn't have to worry about them being sold out and the stock crew would be required for refills less frequently (a major cost savings for the giant retailer).

Whether it was garbage bags or baking products, limiting product selection was a trend, and it wasn't good for those on my side of the negotiation table. The limited space created scarcity of opportunity and dependency—draining our batteries—as the retailers worked to shift us to the dark side of the negotiation spectrum. Our product was being treated as a generic commodity that was interchangeable, so the retailer wasn't dependent on us.

We were expected to participate in this auction, and we were told that only the lowest bidders would be invited in for a follow-up negotiation to iron out the details. The retail giant also required a bunch of mandatory investments, which would mean an even bigger blow to our profitability. Oh, and all questions and communication were to go through this third-party auction company—as they were trying to base the decision solely on price and keep all relationships out of the equation.

Of course, we had some issues with this situation, so I got on the phone with the auction company. They couldn't answer any of my questions (no information-sharing whatsoever—sound familiar?) and redirected me to the buyers. When I called, emailed and left voicemails for the buying team over at the retailer, I received out-of-office notifications and no calls back. Total blackout. I kept leaving messages anyway, explaining that I was happy to discuss investing in their business if we could discuss something that would be more viable for our business together.

A few weeks later, we had done our homework, had run all the numbers, and were faced with the scheduled time for this auction. Based on the math we prepared, our bid was no lower than our current price. It also happened to be the highest starting price, and we bid that way despite being told that we wouldn't even get a meeting to negotiate further if we weren't among the lowest bidders. Yet, a few days later I got an email inviting me in for a meeting (it also included a scolding for not dropping the price). If I had been dealing with a negotiation robot, we wouldn't have been able to step outside of the bounds of the process and rules that were set for this negotiation. There would have been no meeting.

Unlike a robot, I knew that the buyer had listened to my voicemails and read my emails because we picked up where I had left off. A bot wouldn't have been compelled to listen, wouldn't have been able to consider the creative programs we came up with or look outside of the structure that had been set out. Slowly, this other person and I started inching our way toward a more complex negotiation instead of this tunnel-visioned, price-driven one. The product I was representing remained on the shelf (despite our never cutting the price), and we found other ways to work with the retailer to improve the business.

You could chalk up this outcome to the retailer realizing it was dependent on us and the rest of our portfolio of products (I represented more than that one item), or you could say it was our self-control and confidence, or maybe a combination of all of the above. I'm confident it was primarily due to our relationship with the buyer. It made those voicemails and emails possible. It was the reason the buyer was willing to overlook the process and invite me into the negotiation anyway. If we didn't have trust between us, she wouldn't have been willing to risk her credibility by stepping outside of the process and exploring other options with me.

In some ways, our relationships with people are the most influential sources of power. When you're operating with a drained battery, relationships might be just enough to spark a more collaborative conversation and recharge. When you've got a full battery, relationships can be the factor that keeps the other party from wanting to drain it.

HOW LIKABILITY CAN BE PROFITABLE— WHEN USED CORRECTLY

We all have an inherent desire to be liked on some level—we're tribal people, after all. Too often, though, I see people try to buy their likability during a negotiation, thinking that's the way to get it done. That can be costly. If you start getting generous because you want the other party to like you, you're setting a dangerous precedent, and when you can't afford to do what they want in the next negotiation, they'll end up having a meltdown like a two-year-old. While likability can definitely improve your negotiation outcomes, it may not be the way you think.

A series of negotiation studies was conducted between MBA students at two reputable business schools in the US. Some groups were told, "Time is money. Get straight down to business," while others were told, "Before you begin negotiating, exchange some personal information with each other. Identify a similarity you share in common and then begin negotiation."[4]

In the group that got down to business right away, 55 percent of members managed to reach an agreement; in the group that took some time to communicate something in common, 90 percent

closed a deal. Those in the second group also managed to create outcomes that were typically worth 18 percent more to both parties—further proof that pausing and choosing a few extra words to warm up the climate between you can go a long way.

Robert Cialdini, the godfather of all things persuasion and influence, talks about the concept of liking as one of the six principles of persuasion in his many books on the subject, including his first publication, *Influence: The Psychology of Persuasion*. According to him, one of the keys to persuading and influencing others is likability. And we like:

- people with whom we have something in common;
- people who pay us genuine compliments before we get down to business; and
- people who are cooperative.

Start with a common bond, a compliment or a cooperative tone before you move on to your request, and see how much easier it is to get what you want. Sometimes just finding anything in common can help. Likability will get you *to* the negotiation and get you better results by using one of the three elements above, not by giving them everything they want. Likability is an asset *before* the negotiation starts and is as simple as "Those are my favorite pens too!" or "I also prefer chicken over roast beef." *During* the negotiation, focus on being respected and not being taken advantage of. You always need to bear in mind that authenticity is critical when dealing with people. They'll smell a rat if you're lying (remember I mentioned *genuine* compliments above) and if they sense that you're having

some multiple-personality moment that can erode trust and hurt the likability factor instead of helping it. Keep it real and you'll be far more likable.

IF YOU DON'T WANT TO BE SWAYED, KEEP PEOPLE OUT OF IT

We've seen how relationships can significantly enhance negotiation outcomes—an X factor of sorts. If your sole focus is cash, however, and you've got plenty of power, then keeping people out of a negotiation, or minimizing their impact, may be in your best interest.

A friend who recently sold her home told me that her real estate agent refused to tell her anything about the people who were making offers on her house. (At the time of this writing, Toronto has a very hot real estate market, where multiple offers are the norm and the seller has the power to choose the highest bidder.) The reason she was kept in the dark? When the house was being shown, my friend would watch prospective buyers from a neighbor's window. At one point she said, "Ooh, *they* look nice; I want them to get it." Later, when she and the real estate agent were going through the offers and she asked which one belonged to the nice young couple, the agent responded that she wasn't going to reveal that information, because it might distract her from her objective (at the beginning of the process, my friend was clear with her agent that their objective was just to get the highest offer). For that, my friend was grateful.

Given the importance and unpredictability of people, what do we need to keep in mind while preparing for, and during, negotiations?

How do we assess our negotiating partners? We've already talked about trust and relationships. We also need to consider various types of biases (other people's and our own) and find ways to work around them. We need to be aware of how our mindsets and body language affect how others respond to us, and learn to press pause to access our self-control. We need to understand how to define our interests in each negotiation, see how they could align with the other party's interests, and consider the individual we're dealing with and any other stakeholders involved. We also need to recognize that our self-control can be affected by whether we're negotiating for ourselves or someone else.

CHAPTER 11

BIAS: BARRIER OR BENEFIT?

CONTRARY TO POPULAR BELIEF, NEGOTIATIONS ARE NOT conducted via spreadsheets. Facts and formulas are not enough to make people bend to your will. You can't count on the other party believing your assumptions and figures. If we were all operating by the same values and experiences, maybe that would be the case. But we aren't clones of one another (at least not yet), and we bring different experiences and thinking patterns to the table. The other party's riders may not be capable of controlling their elephants, or they may not want to move in the same direction as yours. It's these differences that make an item or issue feel more or less valuable to one party than to another. Our values and experiences evoke emotions in us, and emotions (and elephants) are what rule our thoughts, not spreadsheets. Back in chapter 9, we touched on what commitment bias can do to us when we're playing a slot machine. In this chapter, we'll discuss a few common types of bias and then talk about ways to overcome them, or even use them to your advantage.

ENDOWMENT BIAS

Ever seen something for sale on Craigslist or eBay and wondered why it was priced far higher than you'd expect, given its condition and/or sheer normalness? Maybe you've actually come across some rare and valuable item, but it's more likely the seller is showing the endowment effect: a bias that occurs when we overvalue something we own, regardless of its objective market value. Take my prized George Michael souvenir concert mug. As my friends will attest, I'm a huge George Michael fan and I bought the mug at one of his concerts many years before his death. I used to use it every day to drink my morning smoothie because it was a joyous way to start my day; it brought pleasant memories of my childhood and that concert flooding back. It was well worth the $20 I spent on it.

Someone else who doesn't know who George Michael is, or isn't a fan (is that even possible?), may see the mug solely as a vessel for liquid and worth no more than the dollar it cost to manufacture. And yet, if I were to consider selling it, the positive emotions and nostalgia I get just from seeing that mug in my cupboard might convince me it's worth way more than the original $20. Perhaps more than a hundred (of course, I would never, *ever* sell it). Throw in the fact that George Michael has since passed away and that same mug can never be purchased at a concert again, and it's priceless to me. That's the endowment effect in action—my personal experiences and circumstances overriding spreadsheets and logic. If you come into my home and I let you use my prized possession, you can rest assured that you are pretty special (but a pox on you if any harm should come to it . . . on second thought, maybe you shouldn't use my mug after all).

PREJUDICE

Endowment bias is just one of the many biases we have. We are thinking constantly. Even when you think your mind is blank, at some level, in the depths of your subconscious, your brain is processing thoughts you don't even realize you're having. Based on our experiences, our brains are trained to think a certain way without having to spend energy processing it. Sometimes those biases are there to help us save time or energy: I've had this food before and lived, therefore I'm not allergic to it, so I don't have to worry about consuming it. Sometimes they can ensure our safety: the only dogs I know don't have foam coming out of their mouths, so maybe I won't pet this stray with the foamy mouth. But other times, biases can create some barriers that may prevent us from exploring opportunities and values. If you had a childhood like mine, when you were a kid, you realized—thanks to your early and consistent experiences—that Mom and Dad were a source of comfort, but strangers represented danger. That is a bias that can keep us safe from harm.

Other biases, unfortunately, can be problematic. A manager who consistently only hires one gender or who only promotes people who are similar to him is likely exercising a subconscious bias— "This person is familiar to me and I've had good experiences with this type of person before, so I'm going to hire this similar person again." It is likely that the bias isn't intentional or even something he is aware of; many of us don't recognize our biases until someone points them out. It's as though their elephant mindlessly heads toward people it likes and the rider has managed to rationalize the elephant's direction and thus is operating with blinders on.

We form patterns based on our experiences, as well as the stories that we're told of others' experiences, and at a subconscious level we believe those patterns to be the truth. It's hard to challenge them. Hiring practices and laws are changing all over the place to help ensure that habit and bias don't make us blind to those who aren't familiar to us. So, that hiring manager is now forced to consider candidates who may be a different sex or have a different degree or work experience, and who therefore might open up a new perspective to make the team even better. The rider just looked around and realized there are other directions the elephant could be taking.

HOW THE VIENNA PHILHARMONIC OVERCAME BIAS IN AUDITIONS

One of my favorite examples of overcoming bias at work is the evolution of blind auditions in the Vienna Philharmonic. The orchestra was predominantly male, and yet there were plenty of talented female musicians out there. The orchestra decided to implement blind auditions to increase diversity and ensure that gender wasn't a factor in the selection of musicians, so they had the musicians play their audition pieces behind a screen. Unfortunately, the results still skewed in favor of male musicians. It turns out, our brains are excellent at recognizing the signs of what we are seeking. The sound of the musician walking in was enough to trigger the decision makers' brains to recognize whether a man or a woman was about to audition. When the orchestra switched to blind *and shoeless* auditions, that's when the real change began and almost 50 percent of women made it past the first audition.

Now imagine your brain is thinking about stuff you don't even realize it's thinking about. It's not as if the hiring managers were sitting there, listening carefully and wondering, "Hey, is that a woman's heel or a man's? That person walking in sounds too light to be a man, so let me make sure I don't assess her highly." So, imagine how many things are going through your brain that you don't realize.

TEST YOUR OWN BIAS

Whether we'd like to admit to it or not, our own biases affect the way we think and behave. Awareness of our biases and predispositions can help us prepare for negotiations and help us eliminate blind spots that could be keeping us from creating value. This awareness also makes us much more cognizant of other potential biases that the other party might have.

Think you're free of bias? Test yourself using one of the tests created by Project Implicit, a nonprofit organization of researchers studying social cognition—that is, thoughts and feelings outside of our conscious awareness and control. The tests can be found at **https://implicit.harvard.edu/implicit/**.

Even with all sorts of awareness training, it's hard to break free of bias. Your brain has already formed associations based on your experiences thus far in life, and some of those neural pathways are hard to undo. But that's okay. The first step is to be aware. The ability to press the pause button and challenge yourself every once in a while is an exercise that merits a lot of practice.

WORKING AROUND SOMEONE ELSE'S BIAS

The ability to pause and consider other perspectives is of critical importance in negotiation, not only to prevent your biases from leading you to poor decisions, but also so that you're able to recognize the biases of others. Awareness of the other person's bias is an invaluable skill in negotiation. Some might even call it an advantage.

When I was a teenager, I needed to buy my first laptop in anticipation of going away to university. This was back when laptops were as heavy as cinder blocks and my knowledge of computers was quite limited (truth be told, it still is). So, I asked around and it was recommended that I go to a small local computer store. I had done enough research to figure out the specifications and pricing of a laptop that would meet my basic word processing and web surfing needs, so I went into the shop armed with this information and ready to make a purchase. The few staff members around were male, and they either looked at me as if I had three heads or ignored me. Something was off. I wandered around for some time and wasn't approached at all (unusual, since I was the only customer in the place). Finally, I approached the older guy who was barking orders at the others, clearly the owner, who reminded me a little of my father. He had a thick accent and seemed to come from a similar patriarchal culture to mine. I asked a few questions about what I was seeking and about price points.

When I heard his answers, I paused and decided I wasn't going to make the purchase that day. That familiarity with the culture I was encountering gave me a sense that, as a young woman, I wasn't likely to get the best deal out of this guy. I decided to bring in the big guns: my big fat Greek dad. You should know that to this day, decades later, my father knows nothing about computers. And yet I decided he was better equipped to get a good deal out of this particular computer guy. So, the following day, I went back with him. I had told him exactly what I wanted and the price I was told to expect, and he started the conversation. The two men got on well and the price ended up much closer to what I had anticipated based on my research. At the end of the negotiation, the owner said, "You know, I never would have given you this deal had you come by yourself."

No kidding. My Spidey sense had told me as much. I had recognized his dismissive behavior toward me as part of a pattern of treatment I had seen many times from men in my life, having grown up in a patriarchal culture where most of the women in my parents' social network were relegated to roles more similar to domestic help than true partners in a household.

Clearly, the owner of the computer shop had a bias that caused him to treat men with more respect in the negotiation process than women. And my ability to recognize that was the knowledge I needed to charge my battery. I came with my decoy, my dad, who just became the mouthpiece for my negotiation. I armed him with the proposal and the parameters, and it was better received coming from him than from me. Some might say it's unfair that I had to get my dad to come in and conduct the deal for me. And it is. But my ego was not going to stop me from getting a better deal. This was a one-time negotiation. I didn't need to deal with this person ever again. I wasn't worried about setting a precedent or hurting my future credibility, so I kept my sights on my goal: getting the best possible deal for that single purchase. I was determined that, over the course of the next few years, I would find another vendor who was more aligned with my values and give them my business, but in the short term this guy was my best option.

It was one of my first memories of recognizing bias, and the first where I felt so powerful for having been able to turn it on its head. This was a victory I would reflect on for years to come, and it informed so many of my negotiations going forward. The ability to read this guy's preconception was a lesson I learned from, and continued to build on, for decades. The achievement fueled me to find better and more creative ways to keep overcoming biases (without having to bring in my dad).

Gender bias has reared its head in my life plenty of times since then (along with age, name and many other biases). And the ability to read the other party and assess biases has been the tool I've used to make myself (and my clients) successful instead of a victim. It's the ability to press the pause button and assess the situation and the people we're dealing with that allows us to move in a productive manner instead of wallowing in self-pity or letting anger get the best of us.

Underestimating people can be dangerous. I love it when people underestimate me; I see it as a massive advantage because I have knowledge about my abilities that they don't have. Not knowing who you're dealing with can throw off your whole negotiation strategy. When I met new clients in my early consulting days, I knew they thought I was someone's assistant (I couldn't possibly be the expert they were waiting for). Knowing that I was going to shock the hell out of them when I told them I was their instructor gave me great pleasure and put me in a positive mindset instead of a fearful one. Whenever people underestimate me, they're the ones on their back feet, not me.

I recall sitting in a group interview—I was one of four interviewers—for a new candidate. I was young, of course, and looked nothing like the other interviewers, all of whom were men. The interviewee completely ignored me—assuming I was an intern, I suppose. I bided my time as my battery charged. When the CEO turned to me, saying that I was best poised to answer this candidate's question, you could see the "oh crap" panic moment on his face when he realized that my presence meant something more. At that moment, I had the power to put an end to his career at the company before it started. Instead, I used that power to turn the situation around. I resisted the temptation to lecture him and instead asked questions about how he thought a female client would feel if no one made eye contact with her during a meeting, and how that would affect our ability to gain her trust and her business. We had a very transparent chat about what happened in that room and we even became friends (I know, right?).

If people are underestimating you, they're getting comfortable and complacent and giving you loads of information you can use to charge your battery. Whether they're explaining something you already know or assuming you're the secretary, they are unwittingly giving you power as you take your time to consider your next move. When someone explains a problem I already know the answer to, it's my opportunity to drop in something like "That sounds just like a similar issue I encountered in Yemen." Something to acknowledge them and let them know this isn't my first rodeo.

The ability to *anticipate* the bias is an even more powerful opportunity for you than being able to respond to it in the moment. If you know it's coming, you can find ways to make it work in your favor. If you suspect that the orchestra conductor is going to be biased, then, as with my laptop decoy, get someone they like to send in your audition tape. They'll be anticipating liking your work instead of looking for reasons to dismiss it. When I suspected that I was going to be dealing with age bias at work (all the time), I would make sure that one of my older colleagues had built up my reputation with the potential problem client: "I'm going to send you our manufacturing and retail expert. She works on the highest-stakes scenarios." Before the client had a chance to underestimate me, my colleague's recommendation would change their thought pattern to give me the benefit of the doubt and keep them from trying to drain my battery. If I suspected that they might doubt my experience in the industry, I would be sure to drop the name of a mutual acquaintance whose opinion they respected, so I'd be respected by association (at least enough to get me in the door). Third-party endorsements are a surefire strategy to charge your battery.

One CEO looked absolutely panicked when she saw me walk into her strategy meeting. But when I mentioned our mutual acquaintance's name—"Gerry told me so much about you during our last project together"—I could see her apprehension start to melt away as her fingers stopped nervously tapping on the table and she leaned in to listen to my recommendations.

Bias is such a big part of human nature that its impact on negotiation is impossible to ignore. Pausing to consider the biases of the other party is a huge opportunity to gain power. Knowing a little more about what influences their thinking will inform your plans about how to handle the situation, and as we know, preparation is critical to success in negotiation.

CHAPTER 12

SELF-AWARENESS: FOCUS ON YOU

WE'RE GOING TO SPEND A LOT OF TIME FOCUSING ON THE other party and getting as much of that powerful knowledge as we can. However, the other party isn't the only one at the table with blind spots or emotion-led thoughts. To get the most value from negotiation opportunities, you need to know yourself well. What kind of lens do you typically look at the world through? What pushes your buttons? What helps you stay calm? Where your mind goes will affect how you perform and how others perceive you, so it's critical to get a handle on your thoughts before they have a chance to lead you (and others) astray.

FINDING THE BALANCE

Want to test your self-awareness? To understand a little bit more about your own tendencies, let's do a quick experiment. Using your dominant hand's index finger, draw the capital letter *E* on your forehead. No, seriously. Don't just pretend you did it and keep reading. The people next to you on the train won't notice what you're doing. Done? There are two possible outcomes:

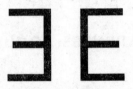

Either you drew this letter so that it makes sense to your eyeballs (like the image on the left), but if I'm looking at you and reading your forehead it doesn't make any sense to me, or you drew it so that I can read it perfectly (the image on the right), but it would look backward to your eyes. *There is no right or wrong answer here*, just an observation about where your brain tends to go first—your autopilot mode. According to Adam Galinsky and Maurice Schweitzer, two American professors, one of these drawings is associated with those who are more powerful (at least in the workplace).[5] They found that the likelihood of creating what an observer like me would see as a reversed *E* (the image on the left) increases with the seniority of the person's role. Thus, more senior or powerful folks are writing the *E* for themselves. Those who wrote it so that others can read it, but it's backward to them (the image on the right), are less self-focused, putting others' needs first. Not surprisingly, women were found to be less self-focused, which is consistent with both what we see in terms of the number of women in senior roles and what I see in my interactions with female audiences.

As I said, and I'm sure other behavioral experts would agree, there is no right answer to this little test, but it is a lesson in self-awareness.

If you're drawing the *E* for yourself, it seems you have a natural tendency to prioritize your own needs; that's how those folks get to achieve their objectives and get to the top of their fields. *However*, I've encountered plenty of folks who will orient the *E* for themselves and still never become the senior leaders they wish to be. Why? They've forgotten what the reflection of that *E* is like—how others are thinking. It's hard to get people to follow you when you're not tapping into something of interest to them.

If you're drawing the *E* for others, you may have a tendency to put others' needs ahead of your own or be more group-focused. If that's the case, ask yourself if you're putting others' needs first *to your own detriment*. Are you desperate to get them to agree or to please them at all costs? That will affect their behavior. Have you factored your needs into the equation, or are you constantly putting them on the back burner for the sake of others? A great leader (and a great negotiator) knows how to use both *E*s to their advantage. They get in charge of their thoughts and affect the other party's behavior.

Make sure you consider your needs, but don't forget about what they need: How would they respond? What would be valuable to them?

Are you constantly putting *them* first? When's the last time you checked yourself and asked, "What am I getting out of this, and what can they afford to do for me?" A key to negotiation success is having the self-awareness to keep this tendency in check when you need to. Throw team dynamics into the mix and you'll find yourself operating on the "we" side of the spectrum, where being able to flip the E to face others is going to be critical to your (and the group's) success. Of course, even on the "we" side of the spectrum, when you grow the pie, at some point you'll still have to divide it up and take your piece—when that time comes, you'll need to flip the E to face yourself, even if only briefly.

Pause to think about your tendency and where you are on the spectrum. How do you need to orient yourself to keep that E in balance? Consider what satisfaction looks like to the other party and how you can build it up to get them to an agreement. Remember that you're not trying to screw the other party over; you're just trying to find an agreement that's going to work for the both of you. The more it works for you, the better. You don't have to give them everything in order to make it acceptable. Check your thoughts and change your behavior.

WHO YOU'RE NEGOTIATING FOR CAN AFFECT YOUR SELF-CONTROL

With this heightened awareness of your own predisposition, you're off to a good start—but there's still another factor to keep in mind. We just finished considering the other party's E and yours, but what if you're not the one, or not the only one, benefiting from this negotiation? What if someone else has to live with the outcome? Are you negotiating on behalf of your boss, spouse, child or others? That might change how much confidence or dependency you have on the other party involved. It may affect how much self-control you're able to exercise.

I can tell you, as someone who is hired to handle negotiations for others, that it's a lot easier to stay in control when it's not your butt on the line. A little bit of distance keeps you objective and allows for plenty of brain capacity for rational thought. There's little threat to you personally, so it's easy to avoid the fight-or-flight instinct. So, if someone had asked me to sell their prized "Who let the dogs out?" mug, I would be able to determine rationally that there is a very small market of people who would care to add this to their collection and the price would have to be close to that functional one-dollar price point.

When you're negotiating for yourself (like those tricky situations at home with your family and significant others), you have more skin in the game and the threat to your values (and your ego) is high (try telling *me* that my George Michael mug is worth only a dollar and I will ice you out for life). That makes self-control so much more difficult. There's a whole load of interesting brain science to explain this, but this book's purpose isn't to get into all that; it's to help you deal with the repercussions of those biological processes. Those knocks to your ego explain why we treat the people closest to us so poorly at times—self-control diminishes rapidly because you are so heavily invested in them that *everything* is personal, it's all a threat to your well-being. Awareness of how these interactions will affect you will help you to devise a strategy before you sit down at the dinner table with those crazy relatives who push your buttons. Maybe you'll plan to start meditative breaths before dinner. Perhaps you need a mantra to remind yourself that it's not about you and your ego, it's about getting the best outcome.

Similarly, if you are going to have a discussion with your child's teacher and are tempted to tell him off because you don't like something he said about your offspring, you could attack his credibility (it will make your ego feel great for a millisecond before you realize that your childish behavior might have made things worse), or you can pause to ask, "How is this helping my child?" Is this going to help them get more out of the classroom experience? Is it going to make it easier for your child to go to school every day? Or will it result in that teacher's residual subconscious resentment and mistreatment of your child? Pausing to remember that your behavior will have consequences for someone else—likely someone you care about if you're putting yourself through this in the first place—will help you channel that self-control.

CHAPTER 13

UNDERSTANDING INTERESTS:
WHAT DO YOU WANT?

WE'VE TALKED ABOUT WHOSE NEEDS WE'RE PUTTING first and whose interests you're serving, but what does that mean? What are "interests" in a negotiation?

Interests are often confused with proposals or demands in a negotiation, so let's get this straightened out first. Your interest is your motivation or the *purpose* you're serving in engaging in the negotiation. It's your objective. The proposal (also called a position) is a *path* to get there. For example, if you're going into a negotiation with your employer, your interest could be better financial security. The proposal to get there could be an increase in salary. It could also be getting your phone or other expenses covered. Maybe a free parking spot or a transit pass. Maybe even a bonus or a relocation fee. Each of those options or proposals will satisfy your interest of increasing your financial security. They each keep more money in your pocket.

Too often we jump ahead and get stuck on proposals without thinking through our actual interests. When you pause to think more strategically about what you're trying to get out of the negotiation, it's much easier to come up with a variety of proposals.

When you're trying to get from point A to point B on a map, if you just draw a straight line between your starting point and your end point, you might be walking through rivers or walls. You'll get stuck. When you enter a destination into any navigation app, it will spit out multiple routes—some longer, some faster, some scenic, factoring in stoplights, traffic jams, construction or road closures. The more options you have, the less likely you are to get stuck.

The same is true in negotiations. The more proposals you have, the easier it is to get to your destination without getting stuck. When you're on the "me" side of the spectrum, there isn't much room for flexibility if all you're doing is chasing the option that gives you the most cash, but as you start looking at other ways to create wealth, you may find some interesting routes to get there. When you zoom out to take a more strategic look at your negotiation, you'll see that there are usually multiple proposals for every interest. The more flexible, open and creative you are in exploring multiple proposals, the easier it will be to find yourself on a path of less resistance.

START WITH WHY

Before you begin any negotiation, you want to make sure you understand what is motivating you. What are you interested in achieving? Avoid the temptation to jump into proposal mode and get stuck there. Pause. Ask yourself what you want and then ask yourself why. Got an answer? Pause. Ask yourself why again. Once you've exhausted your answers so thoroughly that you've got no more *why*s left, you've figured out your motivation. That gives you the opportunity to zoom out of the map to spot all of the possible routes to get there.

Here's an example: Neil is going into a job offer negotiation. He's decided he needs to get a $100,000 salary in this deal. Why? Because he needs more money than he's currently making. Why? Because he needs to be able to pay the mortgage and monthly bills and have some money left over. Why? Because he's worried about retirement and his inability to prepare for it. Neil is looking for long-term financial security. That's his interest. A higher salary is absolutely one way to get him closer to his security goals. But anything that will allow him to tuck away retirement savings will do that. In addition to seeking a higher salary (which he may or may not get), Neil should also be looking for other ways to get to his destination of long-term financial security: matching retirement contributions from the company, moving or transportation costs, cell phone, home office expenses, an equity position or stock options, commission . . . the list goes on. If he had answered that he needed to accumulate cash quickly to put a deposit down on a new place to live, then he might dive a little deeper into proposals for advances, signing bonuses, and anything else that could put money in his pocket in the short term rather than waiting for an end-of-year bonus.

Let's try a different example. Alex wants her partner to take on the afternoon child pickup. Why? She's overwhelmed and needs more help. Why? She's always scrambling to get off work on time, do the pickup, get dinner ready and find some time to take care of herself—whether it's a workout, appointment or just some quiet time. The pickup stresses her out, obviously. Why? Because her afternoons are packed full of too much stuff. Why? Work and traffic are always so crazy and exhausting at that time of day. We can't do much about external forces like traffic, but why is that a problem? The kids are screaming and hangry (hungry leading to angry) because she can't get dinner started fast enough, and it makes for an unpleasant evening that causes her more stress and terrible sleep—an endless cycle. *Phew.* I can understand why Alex is overwhelmed. She needs a little more harmony in her routine; that's her interest (I'm not sure that harmony exists for any parent, but let's go with it). Now, what if the afternoon pickup change isn't the only answer? What if she looked for other shortcuts to harmony, like her partner taking over the morning drop-off so she could get to work earlier and finish a little earlier? How about her partner taking on dinner duties? Or a meal delivery service? An extra snack packed in the child's bag and an extra hour at daycare? With these last few ideas, I'm not suggesting that the partner be excused from helping, but if Alex's partner taking on the pickup duty is going to cause them to lose their job or create additional problems, being open to other creative solutions will be critical.

This is why we don't want to get stuck on one proposal (shifting pickup to the other partner). Doing so could lead to unnecessary conflict and poor communication—a short trip to Resentment Town. Digging deeper into our motivation and identifying our interest will often lead to other proposals that could solve the problem, perhaps even more effectively than the original proposal. Who wouldn't want that?

Another benefit to knowing your Why: it's another way of accessing your pause button before you get entrenched in something that might be serving your ego but not your interest. When that fight-or-flight mode kicks in, it's easy to lose sight of your goal and wind up with a suboptimal outcome. Knowing your Why helps you keep your elephant heading in the right direction.

CHAPTER 14

DO YOUR INTERESTS ALIGN?

YOU KNOW YOUR INTERESTS, RIGHT DOWN TO THE LAST *why*. Are you ready to negotiate now? Not so fast. When you move out of the darkest side of the negotiation spectrum (where you each have the same conflicting interest—generally cash), there are more interests to uncover. Now you need to understand the *other party's* interests, so you can scope out how theirs and yours might be aligned. Negotiations are easier, with better outcomes all around, when you can find common ground.

I've been through a number of real estate transactions in my life, but the most interesting one was my last house purchase. It was set up to be a cold, dark, one-dimensional negotiation, as one usually expects from these deals. It was based on price, the buyers were all anonymous names on paper, and I managed to move it along the spectrum. I happened to meet the owner—let's call her Maria—when I was leaving the space and she was coming home (a fortuitous accident), and we bonded. She saw herself in me, as she was an independent young woman in her thirties when she purchased the house forty years earlier. She was nervous about leaving it and moving to a condo, but her back couldn't tolerate trips up and down the stairs anymore. I reassured her that condo life was great—in fact, I was nervous about leaving my low-maintenance condo for the responsibilities of taking care of a house on my own. I gave her comfort about condo life and listened as she told me the ins and outs of owning this home. She ended by clasping my hand in hers and saying, "If I can do it, you can do it."

Maria and my real estate agent also bonded over their shared love of cats (I stayed out of that one because my allergies and cats don't get along). The morning she was ready to receive our offer, there were three other bids. When the offers were on the table, mine was presented by my agent (as is customary in these parts, I wasn't there), but fortunately, Maria remembered exactly who the agent was and who he represented. We did have more than one round of bidding, with each party being invited back to the table to improve their offers (as anticipated). When it was time for final offers, my agent saw Maria sign a document that signaled that she was turning down the other buyer and accepting my offer. To this day, I'm confident that Maria could have gotten a bit more from the other buyers, but she chose to sell the house to me. She confirmed my suspicion when she got on my agent's phone to tell me that she was happy that I got the place.

Before you start judging her for not getting the maximum price out of this negotiation, you need to understand that her interest wasn't solely the price. So, what were her objectives, and how could I help her meet them?

She wanted to make sure she got enough money to retire comfortably, but we had already surpassed that figure and then some. The financial interest was taken care of. What else was going on?

It was obvious from the care she'd taken of the house that she took great pride in it. She was reluctant to leave and was selling only because her body didn't want her to stay. What would make the transition easier? Not having to sever all ties. By being willing to help her maintain a connection to the neighborhood and to invite her back to the home, I served her interest in staying connected to her home of forty years. (A couple with a newborn was unlikely to invite her over for tea or invest the time in the email exchanges that we did leading up to and after the move.)

Going into any negotiation, you've got to be able to identify your objective as well as the other party's. For most people, a real estate sale is about price and nothing more. Case in point: when I sold my condo two weeks later, I didn't care who bought it or what they wanted to do with it; I just wanted the highest price. For others, it's about more than that. Maybe it's important for them to be able to drive by when they want a dose of memories and nostalgia, so they don't want their home to be replaced with a parking lot. Everyone is going to be different. Some people, like the buyer of my condo, are willing to pay more for a quick move-in date because one of his interests was that he not have to couch-surf while in between homes. Others, like me, would be happy to put their things in storage for a few weeks in between moves to get a better price. I was on the road every week with clients and I saw it as an opportunity to spend the weekends visiting family.

In negotiations that aren't solely about cash, it's hard to know what people truly want. We take what people say at face value, but we need to dig a little deeper to resolve most disagreements with ease. For example, I go to a lovely Pilates studio for regular classes in a small group. The only problem is that the room is freaking warm every time I go. It drives me nuts. Imagine going to a hot yoga studio and then start throwing in resistance training and crunches. There are some people who love hot, sweaty studios. I am not one of them. So, for a long time, I would ask the instructor to turn on the air conditioning when I came in. It got to the point where I didn't have to ask; she would turn it on as soon as she saw me walk in the door (one of the many reasons I adore her).

But then another woman who came in didn't like the air conditioning and got uncomfortable. This situation could have turned into an awkward exchange for the instructor, who was torn between satisfying two very different clients in the same class. Fortunately, I shared this piece of information with her: I have a long history of fainting when the temperature is too hot or the air circulation is poor. (Doctors haven't been able to figure out why, but it served as a convenient "get out of church free" card whenever I was bored or uncomfortable, since that seemed to be the place where it happened most.) Sharing my interest in better circulation allowed for a clever solution of turning on a fan right next to my machine; the fan didn't affect the other woman at all and negated the need for the air conditioner's cold air. Problem solved.

How did we avoid getting into a catfight or make the poor instructor feel like a monkey in the middle (can I throw in any *more* animal metaphors)? First, the Pilates community is a lovely bunch of people, but anyone can get triggered under the right circumstances. Second, I gave the instructor a vital piece of information to solve the issue: the reason I wanted the air conditioning on. I wanted better air circulation to make sure I didn't get dizzy, or worse, pass out.

Turning on the AC was one way of managing that problem, but it wasn't the only way. Pointing a fan in my direction was also a way of making sure I wasn't going to fall on my face and break my nose. Another option: opening the window and assigning me the machine next to it, and assigning my peer the machine farthest away from it. I would avoid getting sick (my interest) and my peer would avoid getting cold (her interest). The fan, pointed directly at me, seemed to be the optimal solution, particularly in the winter months, to make sure that the cold air didn't spread across the room.

The key is that there are multiple ways to solve for the interests—but you must understand what those interests are; otherwise, you'll be spinning your wheels making proposals that don't solve the actual problem. We could have compromised by having the AC on for half of the class and off for half of the class, but then you'd just have two people who are uncomfortable for some period of time. Scratch beneath the surface and you'll find that you can often discover an interest that has a corresponding position to serve both parties.

There's one more factor here: framing my interest in a way that aligns with the other party's. Saying only "I need the air to circulate" could elicit yawns and "who cares?" responses. But stating the real problem *and* framing it in terms of the instructor's interests—"I don't want the class to be disrupted if the air starts making me sick"—gets their buy-in right away.

A conversation about interests will prevent a lot of discomfort and potential conflict. But even if the conflict has started and you've heard the dreaded no, then instead of shutting down, pause to consider how this could be the start of digging a little deeper to find a solution.

CHAPTER 15

WHO AM I DEALING WITH?

YOU'VE DETERMINED YOUR INTEREST IN THE NEGOTIATION and you recognize that there are multiple ways to achieve that interest. Great. But the conversation isn't going to go anywhere yet. Why? Well, there are two parties in this negotiation, and to solve this one, you'll need to focus on the most important one . . . *them*.

Now, you know I'm all about helping you get what *you* want, but you can't do that until you factor the other party into the equation. If you have to deal with them to get what you want, then you have to consider what they want.

Let's be clear: considering the other party's needs and interests does *not* mean throwing yours out the window. This is often the temptation for those who want to ensure harmony or desperately want to be liked—"I don't want to upset anyone, so I'll just forget about my needs this one time and give them what they want." Be careful that you don't fall into this trap (remember, Our Way still has to include you). There's a reason I've made you consider what *you* want first. That's why you're reading this book. Factoring in their needs is a tool to plot a more efficient route toward getting what you want. And if what you want is a fair outcome, then that's okay as long as it's fair to you too.

If it's a My Way negotiation and this person or group is the only thing standing in the way of your getting what you want, then you had better know enough about them to figure out how to get around or through them. That doesn't mean yelling at them or beating them up until they bend to your will—even when you have all the power, that often doesn't work. Some people would rather suffer than give you what you want if you approach them in a way that makes that fight-or-flight mode kick in. Rational thought disappears, the elephant takes over, and they prepare to fight you the whole way. They may not be as adept at pressing their pause button, which means you need to be prepared to help them to do that and guide their elephant back into line with the rider.

After spending some time thinking about what it's like in their shoes, you may even find yourself with the opportunity for an Our Way negotiation. You could find ways to align your interests and come up with some creative solutions. How? Well, once you've considered your why (remember, this is the goal after all), consider the person you're dealing with. We've touched on a few things to consider, but here is a reference list to tuck away as you prepare for your next negotiation:

- Why are they here talking to you right now? They need something from you in order to serve some objective. What is it that they need?
- What kinds of pressures are they facing? What are the consequences if they don't reach an agreement?

- Who do they represent? Who is the stakeholder who owns the outcome or is affected by the outcome? Your negotiating partner may merely be the conduit for someone who's actually making the decisions. Consider the other players who may be involved.
- Who might be influencing the stakeholder's decision?
- How much power does the other party have? Consider what you could do to drain their battery or charge yours.
- What perception do they have of you? That can affect the balance of power between you and how you may need to approach your strategy.

If you're dealing with a mortgage agent at the bank, consider what they're trying to accomplish. They probably want to make sure they sign another customer with the bank. They want to ensure that they hit their monthly quota. And maybe they want a quick win to look good to their boss. Your ability to make them look good charges your battery and creates a dependency that would drain theirs. Perceptions become reality in their mind. Do they think you're someone who knows your stuff? Do they think you've come in without doing your homework and are thus likely to accept a bad rate on a mortgage instead of the lowest advertised price? Do they think you're a high-risk borrower, which would make them reluctant to give you what you want for fear of it coming back to bite them later? How can you manage their expectations and change the conversation to your advantage? You could signal that you've been talking to other banks or doing some research online. Their perception would then change: now you're a credible customer they don't want to upset and to whom they're going to have to offer a competitive rate.

If you're considering going to speak to your child's teacher about some unmet needs, you'll want to spend some time thinking about what it's like to be in his shoes. Perhaps he needs this meeting to go smoothly so that he doesn't get a complaint. Or maybe his objective is to get you to see that everything he's doing is in your child's best interest. Perhaps he's following instructions from the principal or curriculum advisor and is not authorized to meet your requests. If that's the case, this person has no power and this discussion won't get you what you want. You may find yourself realizing that it's the principal you need to speak to. The teacher could, however, be a *source* of power as he gives you the knowledge you need to conduct a fruitful conversation with the real decision maker. Demonstrating up-to-date knowledge of the curriculum would make the principal perceive you as a highly engaged parent rather than one who is uninformed and is wasting their time.

Of course, going back to Sasha and her job offer success story, pausing to focus on what's going on inside the other party's brain and the pressures they're facing is always a valuable exercise. It will give you the knowledge and confidence you need to take your next step. So remember, ask yourself, "What kind of pressures are they facing? What are the consequences if they don't reach an agreement?" You'll notice I didn't ask what the consequences were for *you*. It's safe to assume your brain went there a long time ago without my prompt. That's the reality of the fear associated with negotiation—we go to our worst case easily. You know your fears; don't dwell on them. Focus on the fears those other folks might have.

What do they stand to lose if this agreement falls through? What are those BATNAs we talked about earlier? All of these are factors that you need to build into your negotiation strategy.

As you consider the individuals you're dealing with, you're going to want to consider their overall mindset *as well as* the one you need them to be in for you to get what you want. What can you do before the negotiation starts to get them into the headspace you need them to be in? If you need them to think collaboratively and behave as though there's some trust between you, what can you do to create the environment or the climate that would make them want to open up? You may want to start with some words of positive intent that highlight a mutual why, such as "We both want the child to get the best education."

Do you need them to be nervous or scared so that you can satisfy a My Way negotiation quickly? How can you set up a cold climate that would cause them to feel somewhat intimidated? You may want to share that you're not thrilled about the service you've been getting from the bank lately and you've started to explore other options. That will certainly stir up some fear across the table if they know they need to keep you as a client. Be careful of misinterpreting cold for rude. There's never a need to be rude or insulting to people. You can get what you want without having to burn bridges, and civility will not make you look weak.

CONSIDERING OTHER STAKEHOLDERS IN A NEGOTIATION

While you might be physically in the room with another person in your negotiation, it's important to recognize that there are often other stakeholders to take into account. As I mentioned earlier, consider who the person sitting in front of you might be representing or who else may be influencing them. These are folks that have some kind of vested interest in the discussion—maybe it's a financial stake; maybe they're the ones who have to live with the consequences of the discussion. Don't confuse real stakeholders with the loudmouths who just happen to have strong opinions and like to hear the sound of their own voices. You can't please everyone, but you do need to consider the ones who have a direct link to this negotiation.

I'm not much of a sports fan, but a sports analogy[6] works well here, and since I'm Canadian and the Raptors were the reigning NBA champions at the time of this writing, let's talk about basketball. The five players on the court who comprise one of the teams are there to execute the plays. They're out there, scoring all of the points, and they obviously have a huge interest in achieving the team's goals. They're the negotiators at the table in this analogy, but they've been hired by someone else who is even more heavily invested. If the players go rogue and stop following the coach's instructions, they could get cut or traded. On the sidelines, the coach is diagramming the plays, looking out for the well-being of the entire team, and making decisions at a more strategic and tactical level, with more overall knowledge than each of the individual players on the team.

The coach is also serving the needs of the owner of the team. The owner is sitting in a luxury box nowhere near the court, but he is the one allocating the budgets and authorizing the coach and general manager to make key decisions. He knows that he's not completely up to date on the everyday activities of the team; he has to delegate that responsibility to the guys in the front office and on the sidelines, but they know he has the authority to veto their decisions at any time. Then, of course, there are the spectators. They make a lot of noise and may have some emotional attachment to the team's performance, but they don't get a say in any of the team's decisions, and even though they may claim that they have to live with the consequences, they don't have any skin in the game.

When I'm in the war room helping clients with their negotiations, we always have a challenging discussion about who the stakeholders and key decision makers are in the situation. We dig deep to figure out who's managing the situation from the sidelines and start plotting a strategy to engage the appropriate stakeholders—directly or indirectly.

Of course, when you're negotiating, you also have to ask yourself: Are you a player, or are you the owner? Are you out there on your own, or are there other people's interests that you have to consider? Is it possible you may have forgotten about your stakeholders? When you're thinking about that meeting with your child's teacher, your child owns the outcome of that discussion. They have to pass the decision-making on to you, but they are going to have to deal with the consequences, so you need to consider their interests.

I'm not suggesting that you start overcomplicating and overthinking each of your negotiations; some of them are going to be simple, involving you, the person across from you, and no one else. You don't need to worry about anyone else when you're buying elephant pants in Thailand. But there will be other occasions where you're going to have to exercise some self-control and consider the needs of those others (whether they're on the court or on the bench) before you go rogue and lose sight of the fact that others are depending on you.

PAUSE FOR REFLECTION

SECTION 3 | PEOPLE OVER SPREADSHEETS
CHECKLIST OF KEY TAKEAWAYS

✓ **People are so important they get their own section!** They can move you along the spectrum, so you'll need to factor them in or out of your plan in order to keep your battery from draining.

✓ **Likability is a negotiation asset.** People prefer to say yes to those they like, and likability can be profitable if used correctly *before* the negotiation.

✓ **Bias can have a dramatic effect.** We all think differently, and bias can rule our decisions at a subconscious level. Being aware of our own biases and using the knowledge of the other party's biases can be a source of power instead of a disadvantage.

✓ **Know yourself—your tendencies, your triggers.** Self-awareness is the first step to success. Once you know what makes you tick (or what ticks you off), you can prevent things from going wrong by using coping mechanisms and preparing effectively.

✓ **Flip the *E* both ways.** A great negotiator (and leader) knows how to balance their self-interests and consider the interests of others.

- ✓ **Understand the difference between your interests and proposals.** You don't want to get stuck on a position that could be preventing you from getting what you want.
- ✓ **Factor in interests.** As you move along the spectrum, interests are less about cash and more about the value you can create. Try to find a way to align interests if you're in an Our Way scenario, and you'll encounter a lot less resistance.
- ✓ **Who are you dealing with?** Where are they coming from? You need to know the landscape in order to figure out the route to get to your destination.
- ✓ **Who else do you have to consider?** Don't forget about the other people in the negotiation—they may not even be in the room, but they can still have a significant influence.

SECTION 4

THE PROCESS MY WAY:
THE COMPETITIVE SIDE

CHAPTER 16

CHOREOGRAPHING SATISFACTION

I DON'T KNOW WHAT IT IS ABOUT THE CHILDREN IN MY life—or maybe it's all kids in this age group—but my nieces and godchildren have always liked playing with tiny toys: Shopkins, Lego, building blocks, cars, figurines, you name it. My seven-year-old godson has always been into little collectibles, but I've always tried to shy away from buying him gifts with lots of pieces. I was always conscious of what kind of gifts I would bring him so as to not contribute to the chaotic result of a few minutes of play. Have you ever tried to get a little kid to pick up their toys? They rarely do so willingly, and with his mom being one of my dearest friends, I have no interest in adding to her torture or stepping on one of the dreaded rogue pieces and trying to control the curse words that would inevitably come out of my mouth. But she always has brilliant hacks at the ready to get him to tidy up—for example, issuing a challenge like "There's no way you can put all of your toys away before I can finish the dishes." And off he'll go, motivated to prove her wrong. I often follow with something like "You put that all away by yourself? Are you *sure* you didn't get any help?"

Rising to the challenge or announcing with pride that he had done it unaided would always be accompanied with a big grin and a sense of satisfaction. His mom could just give him orders to clean up before my arrival; it would seem to be more efficient than conjuring up a game. And I could ignore his efforts without acknowledging the energy I knew he put into it—it was expected that he would clean up after himself, after all, and I'm not one of those adults who advocates for giving participation ribbons for baseline efforts. But the minimal extra effort we put forth made the task of cleaning up so much more satisfying for him and prevented a lot of the resistance you often see with kids.

Which option sounds more appealing: delivering an extra line of dialogue to create some satisfaction, or dealing with the whining that comes with giving a child orders to do something they don't want to do?

You may think, "Sure, we play mind games with kids, but that wouldn't work with adults." Fact is, the choreography that we go through as adults shows up all the time. If you're anywhere in North America, you'll notice that adults greet each other with "Hi, how are you?" when they don't actually expect you to give them an update on your last physical. They do it because it's part of the rituals and motions we go through to create a little more satisfaction for the other person. We're likely to be perceived as rude by not asking or replying with a "Fine, thanks." We could just skip the routine and not acknowledge each other, but eliminating this greeting would make for a much less pleasant interaction. The extra few words have an impact on how people respond to you. When I get to a cash register as a customer, I expect the cashier to ask, "How are you?"

but they're always a little taken aback and extra pleasant when I ask *them*. It makes for a more satisfying transaction for both of us.

These rituals impact us in subtle ways. They take minimal effort, but engaging in them makes interactions a little smoother. The same is true in negotiation. I can go into any negotiation and ignore the rituals we expect and start demanding what I want or getting straight to the point, but it's going to make for a much more challenging conversation. I compare it to getting on the dance floor with someone. If you've ever watched two skilled dancers, they move effortlessly across the floor, from one end to the other, because they follow a choreography that helps move them along efficiently. Take two amateurs who don't know what dance they're dancing, and they'll be tripping over each other and stumbling their way across the floor—if they even make it to the other side without injury. There's nothing efficient about that, it's just one hurdle or bruise after another.

So, although some may think, "But we don't need to do these silly dances—we can just get straight to the point," I implore you to think about some of the rituals you've come to expect and what your reaction is like when your barista doesn't greet you before taking your order. Imagine how the attitude or feeling that is evoked can impact the outcome of the conversation when the stakes are higher than the thirty seconds you have to deal with that person.

Depending on where you are on the negotiation spectrum, these rituals can look a little different. On the darker side, they center on a choreographed set of numbers or trades, a process we're about to explore in great detail. On the lighter side, they primarily take the form of communication techniques that demonstrate acknowledgment and trust to create progress. As is the case with everything on this side, things are more complex and less tangible, but when you break it down, there are some easy ways to keep people satisfied and working toward solutions that work for everyone.

On both sides, we need to prepare for the dance. We need to know which moves we're going to need to have in our repertoire to get across the dance floor and create enough satisfaction to get the other party to keep dancing until we get what we want. On the dark side, we can break down the steps that will create satisfaction through a simple template.

CHAPTER 17

PREPARING FOR THE DARK SIDE:
A ROAD MAP FOR SUCCESS

WHENEVER I'M COACHING STUDENTS OR CLIENTS ON preparing for any type of negotiation, I urge them to fill out a planning document (well, I *force* my MBA students to fill them out by making it a component of their final grades!). It's a habit that they recognize contributes to their success, so much so that I regularly get updates from former students and clients telling me that they still prepare planning documents on a regular basis—even for their negotiations at home. The planning document for these transactional negotiations is straightforward. On a page, I have them fill out the following:

- My issues (in order of importance)
- Their issues (in order of importance)
- My power sources
- Their power sources
- My resistance point
- Their resistance point (my target)

- My move plan—proposals
- Their opener—their aspiration
- Questions I may need to ask
- Other considerations

This planning document introduces terms we haven't discussed yet, like *resistance point* and *move plan*, but we'll go through each section of the plan in the order in which you'll be filling it out to prepare for your negotiations.

The order here is important. You need to pause to make sure you're considering your needs first and decide what you want out of this transaction. Then you have to flip that *E* around to consider what their mentality and strategy will be. This will not only help you determine which dance moves to use to get what you want, but it will also prevent any surprises from throwing you off your plan. It's like inserting pause buttons before you even need them. This is one of the many reasons why this adage rings true: an ounce of prevention is worth a pound of cure.

Pausing to take the time to prepare for a negotiation may seem tedious to you, especially when there's only price on the table to discuss, but I *guarantee* you'll appreciate those few minutes that you paused instead of having the deer-in-the-headlights moment when they say something that prompts all of that energy to leave your brain and leaves you stammering as you try to figure out what to do or say. Not only will those moments be less likely, thanks to your anticipating them in advance, but you'll also have the safety net of having thought through your answers to those moments of panic. Dancing circles around them will be much easier if you

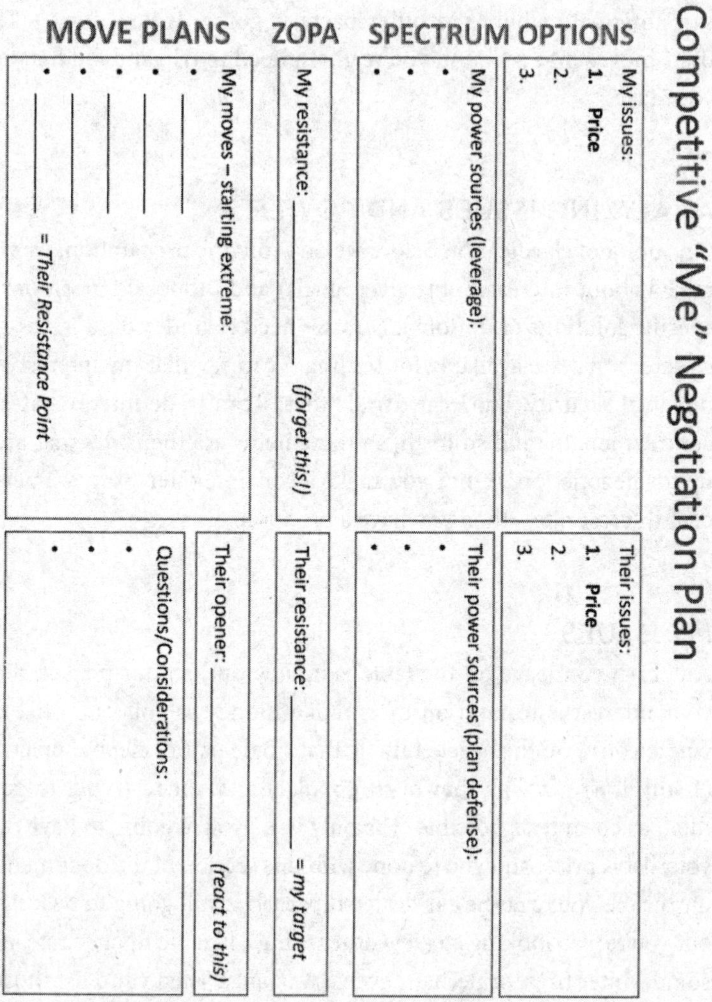

Competitive "Me" Negotiation Plan

MOVE PLANS   ZOPA   SPECTRUM OPTIONS

My issues:
1. **Price**
2.
3.

My power sources (leverage):

- • • • •

My moves — starting extreme:

- • • • • •

= Their Resistance Point

My resistance: _____

(forget this!)

Their issues:
1. **Price**
2.
3.

Their power sources (plan defense):

- • • •

Their resistance: _____

= my target

Their opener: _____

(react to this)

Questions/Considerations:

- • • • •

Figure 3: The competitive negotiation planning document to fill out before any "me" negotiation.

can anticipate where the other party is going. If you don't take their moves into account, you're guaranteed to trip and fall flat on your face.

ANALYZING ISSUES AND POWER

One point of clarification before we dive into the preparation: we've talked about interests (objectives, goals) and proposals (positions, specific solutions or options). Now we need to understand *issues*— variables that are available for trading. I can say that my interest is financial security, but I can't trade that. I can trade interest rates, contract length, and so forth, so these items are the *issues* that are up for negotiation. (Once you make a concrete offer—say, a 2 percent interest rate—then you have a proposal.)

MY ISSUES

Any cash you leave on the table is money out of your pocket. So, your interest is to hold on to as much money as you can. This is where you're on the beach, buying that single pair of elephant pants (I still don't get why they're so popular) and you're trying to get them as cheaply as possible. The only issue you're going to have on your list is price, and you're done with this section of the document. Or maybe you're at the car dealership; cash is still going to be king, but you're also looking at a few other things, like the finance rate, or some winter tires, or perhaps even a warranty. Then you'd list those items in order of importance to you.

YOUR ISSUES
1. Price
2. Finance rate
3. Warranty
4. Winter tires
5. Fancy floor mats

Why is it so important to be this organized on your planning sheet? Because if the going gets tough and you're not getting everything you want on your big wish list, you'll be able to quickly assess where to focus your time and energy. You don't want to spend twenty minutes arguing with the salesperson over a free oil change worth $50 when you could be working to improve the sale price or the interest rate— elements that could save you hundreds, if not thousands, of dollars.

As you start to list your priorities, it's a good time to do a little inventory check and decide whether this still is a "dark" negotiation or if you've found a way to make it more complex and intangible. If price is still far outweighing all of your needs, don't kid yourself and try to make this an Our Way negotiation. If price moves down the list, then reevaluate and start preparing for a more complicated, creative, lighter negotiation.

WHAT ARE THEY THINKING?—THEIR ISSUES

Often, when I'm running exercises with my students, they'll tell me, "But I don't know what they're thinking, I'll find out when I get in there." That's just too damn late. And it isn't all that crazy an expectation. It's generally easy to suss out what is important to someone by just spending a moment in their shoes. If you were the elephant pants vendor, it's easy to determine that they want to sell their stuff and do it quickly so that they don't have to spend more time roasting in the sun and carrying around a heavy load of products. If it's the car dealer, you know they want to get the best price, and they wouldn't mind roping you in for financing, because they stand to make even more money off of the interest you'll pay for that loan. Is it the end of the month? That might mean that this person is eager to make their quota. Are you there in the fall, when dealers are trying to clear the lots to make room for next year's models? Perhaps that means they're eager to get rid of the car you're looking at.

THEIR ISSUES

1. Price
2. Finance rate
3. Timing; get that car sold quickly

With all of this in mind, you can now anticipate some of the things that are going to come up in conversation (or that you can use to your advantage) and plan some proposals. If you've never thought before about the cost of financing, you don't want to be caught off guard and trying to do math in your head while you're standing in the showroom. And you'll want to know if you're ready to take possession of the vehicle right away or if you're still in the early stages of shopping around. Have you done all of your homework on what's out there yet? You can use the dealer's eagerness to your advantage if you're prepared.

MY POWER SOURCES
(HOW CHARGED IS MY BATTERY?)

Here's another area we discussed at length in an earlier section. Before you get into this negotiation, you want to think about what-if scenarios. If, for some crazy reason, you can't work out a deal with this person, what is your next best option? You want to be able to identify your best alternative to the negotiated agreement ahead of time, because it helps you to determine how dependent you are on this individual. You don't want to find yourself walking away from this negotiation, with nowhere else to go, if it's still possible to reach a deal with this person. On the flip side, if you're getting a suboptimal deal here, it's easy to justify moving on to your next option. You shouldn't agree to a terrible deal if there's even a slightly better one waiting in the wings. Thinking things through in advance will help you pause to find some clarity should things get difficult.

You'll also want to note any other sources of power you're bringing to the table. What can you leverage? How can you give yourself a confidence boost before you go in? Pause to think about why the other party needs to engage with you. Assessing your power will not only build your confidence but also help you to justify how demanding you can be in this negotiation. If you're the only option the other person has, that's enormously powerful and you can demand a lot more.

If you're going to a car dealer, you may realize that you are one of the few people in town who's willing to buy a bright purple car (no judgment here). Or if you're buying from someone who placed an ad saying that they're looking to make a quick sale because they're moving out of the country (I've seen this mistake before), you know that their time pressure and your lack thereof could work in your favor and make them want to come down to your figure.

MY POWER SOURCES

1. I've got no time pressure—buses, ride-sharing and car rentals are all viable options for the next few weeks

2. I'm not picky about color, so I can look for something else

3. They're desperate for cash, and I have it!

BATNAs: other dealers in the area, online sellers

THEIR POWER SOURCES (HOW CHARGED IS THEIR BATTERY?)

While we're on the subject of the other party, let's hang out here for a few more minutes and think about what kind of power they have. What do I need to anticipate, and perhaps neutralize, before we get started? What are they going to try to use to make me nervous and increase my dependency on them?

When you're buying those elephant pants, is the seller going to try to convince you that he's the only one with this particular fabric and print (so they're worth more than those sold by the guys down the beach)? Do you really care about that for a pair of pants you will probably never wear again after you get back on the plane to go home?

Will the car dealer tell you he's had multiple people looking at that same car in the last few days, putting time pressure on you to act quickly? If you anticipate that, you might be prepared to say something to the effect of "Then why haven't they bought it?" to neutralize the power or turn the tables. Perhaps he'll say something about how it's the only model he's seen with a particular set of features (low mileage, color, upgraded sound, etc.) in a long time, so you should jump on it. If you have thought about these predictable sources of power in advance, you can pause to recall you're not in a rush, so you don't have a problem waiting for the next one to come around.

THEIR POWER AND BATNA
1. Other buyers
2. Unique model

How does your power measure up to theirs? Who has a stronger battery? What can you do to drain their battery and beef up yours? This is the time to be asking yourself these questions to make sure you've got not just the right data, but the right mindset to get in the game.

PLANNING AHEAD:
UNDERSTAND RESISTANCE POINTS

So, you've thought through where you're going to go if this deal doesn't work out, but how do you know when to pull the chute and get the heck out of there? The *resistance point*, also known as the *reservation price*, is the least acceptable deal you are willing to make before you resist making a deal at all. It's the last point before you walk away and head to your BATNA.

MY RESISTANCE POINT (HOW FAR CAN I GO?)

Identifying your resistance point *before* a negotiation is essential. You don't want to be deciding when to walk away when your brain is under a lot of stress, and you don't want to find yourself wondering, "Why did I do *that*?" later, so here's a golden opportunity to prevent some big regrets. Trust me: when you're focusing on calming your nerves during the negotiation and your brain isn't working with its full rational capacity, you won't "just know" your resistance point intuitively. Say you're one of those nuts who likes to jump out of airplanes. You know that to safely land on your target, you need to open your parachute when you're within a certain range of altitude. Opening the chute too early might get you a long, cold ride as you drift far away from the drop zone, and waiting too long could be disastrous. Are you going to depend on your intuition to tell you when you've hit the right range—or when you've reached the lowest possible safe altitude? No, you'll use an altimeter. You might even program it to sound a warning beep in case you get too entranced (or terrified) by the amazing view.

Likewise, before you go into your negotiation, you need to determine your worst-case scenario. The lowest or highest you'll go. The line you draw in the sand. The last straw. And any other cliché I can think of that says that this is the last step that is acceptable to me. Any steps further and I'm better off walking away toward my BATNA.

The most common mistake I see when people try to determine their resistance points is that they confuse them with their targets. If the resistance point is your worst-case scenario, that is not where you're *trying* to go; it's where you're trying to *avoid* going unless you have to. That's why I'm always quick to point out the difference between a worst-case and a nice-to-have. If it's nice, then you won't mind heading there and settling for it quickly. If it's the least acceptable option to you, then you won't be in a rush to settle there. If I could, I would put my resistance point in one of those glass boxes that say "In case of emergency, break glass." Unless it's an emergency, one that would require you to go to a BATNA that will leave you worse off, then you're not going to touch it. Sometimes you have to go there because your BATNA just isn't as good as what's in that glass box, but you're sure as hell going to put a plan together that will put every effort into not having to break that glass. It's like having a bank account solely for a rainy day fund. You don't start using that money to pay your daily bills. It's separate, and out of sight, in case you need to withdraw it someday. There's no shame in using it, but it is a last resort.

Just please, for goodness' sake, *don't ever tell the other party your resistance point*! Divulging this sensitive piece of information is the next most common mistake I see. You wouldn't tell a mugger about the extra cash you've got hidden in your shoe, so don't tell your competitive counterpart about your emergency stash.

In a basic negotiation, where only price is on the table, all you have to do is decide how much you are willing to spend before it doesn't make sense anymore. If you know that the average seller is letting the elephant pants go for $12, then why would you pay any more than that? It doesn't make sense. Your resistance point would therefore be $12. If the vendor you're speaking to insists that he needs more than $12, your resistance point, then it's time to walk away and head toward your BATNA down the beach.

With negotiations that may have a couple of other items in the mix, you're going to have to factor in the total package's reservation value. If you're buying a car and you're only considering price, then you'll go through a similar decision-making process. Maybe you determine your worst case by how much you can afford: how much you're going to borrow, how much the monthly payments are going to cost you, and how many months you want to use to pay off the loan. Maybe you've decided that you can only afford to spend up to $500 per month for this car for the next twelve months. After that, you're going to have some additional expenses (mortgage, tuition, baby, vacation) and you can't afford to keep laying out cash for this car. So that means your breaking point is $500 for twelve months, or $6,000 in total. If you're financing the purchase, you'll have to calculate the interest on the loan and deduct that from the $6,000 you have to spend—the remainder is the maximum sticker price you can afford to pay. If you can't get the car for that total outlay of $6,000, you'll have to go to your BATNA—which might be a car you don't like as much, or begging your friends and family for rides, or waking up earlier to take the bus that you hate.

But what about those winter tires you know you're going to need? If the seller doesn't include them with the car and you have to go out and buy them on your own, it's going to cost you $500 for new ones. Ugh. Now you've only got $5,500 to spend on the car (and the interest). But if the seller has some lightly used snow tires that they aren't going to use any more anyway, then you've got the whole $6,000 to spend. You've just figured out a total package reservation value.

We talked earlier about salary negotiations and how they can have both tangible and intangible factors. While they fit farther along the spectrum in a lighter area, we're going to have to figure out a reservation value for the total compensation. If you know that in order to take this job, you need to be able to accomplish all of your current financial goals, you're going to use that to determine the reservation value of your total compensation package. Let's say that to meet your objectives (paying your bills and putting a certain amount toward savings every month), you need to earn $5,000 per month, or $60,000 per year. However, out of that $5,000, you're taking $300 a month to pay for parking at work. If your new employer is offering a complimentary parking pass, then you can accept $4,700 a month. If they're offering to cover your cell phone, commuter tolls, association fees or other expenses, then you can accept even less. The key is to know your numbers, so that you can determine whether the offer exceeds your total reservation value.

THEIR RESISTANCE POINT
(HOW FAR WILL THEY GO?)

You've got your emergency plan ready and you think you're ready to go, but hold on. What do you think the other party would be willing to accept before *they* resist making a deal and walk away to their BATNA? What does their worst-case scenario look like? How low or high do you think they'd be willing to go if they had to? This is not to be confused with a point that they would be happy or cool with going to. It's their "in case of emergency, break glass" point.

I know you don't have a crystal ball, but you have enough insight and common sense to take a stab at it. If everywhere you've gone, you've seen elephant pants for an average of $12—with a seller in the next town over offering them as low as $10—then it's a no-brainer to assume that $12 is acceptable to the seller you're dealing with. But that might not be their worst case . . . are there circumstances under which you think they might go lower? What if it were the end of the day and the vendor is just tired of carrying his stuff around and is willing to just unload his final pair? What if he's sitting on so much stock, he doesn't know how he's going to get rid of it all? What if it's been raining all day and you're the first tourist he's seen? Perhaps, feeling like his battery is a little drained, he might be willing to accept as little as the lowest price on the market—maybe even less than $10. Why not try for $9? Or $8? Use your gut instincts and your specific circumstances to decide what feels appropriate.

You want to be careful to stay realistic, but for those who are generally uncomfortable with hard bargaining, I would proffer that you're likely going to err on the side of being too realistic (or generous) rather than unrealistic. If you put yourself in the other person's shoes, where is the lowest *you* would be willing to go? That is their resistance point. It's the most important piece of quantitative data you can have when you go into "dark" negotiations.

Sometimes, there may be more than one resistance point or total package resistance point. In our car-buying scenario, the dealer's resistance point could be slightly lower than the average price on the market. If the average for this car is $6,000, then maybe you could get it for $5,400. And if you're getting financing, you've also got to consider the resistance point for the interest rate. Is the average interest rate 2 percent? How much lower than that are your gut instincts telling you this could go before they walk away, resisting making a deal with you? Perhaps it's 1.6 percent. Maybe that's a tiny bit lower than their next closest competitor, and that's the size of the hit they'd be willing to take to prevent you from taking your business there.

THEIR RESISTANCE POINT

$5,400 price

1.6 percent interest

Once again, you need to have done your homework to find out what information is out there in the universe to help you get inside this person's head. If you were in their shoes, what would you accept? Of all of the pieces of information on this planning document, this one is by far the most important.

THE ZONE OF POSSIBLE AGREEMENT

Once you've determined your resistance point and theirs, you've identified where a deal can take place: the zone of possible agreement, or ZOPA (see figure 4). Somewhere between your resistance point and theirs, there is a deal that can be made. If your max is $12 and they need to recover their costs at $7, then somewhere between (and including) $7 and $12 there is a point where you could each agree. You may not know that yet, and you may not be willing to do it right away, but it's within the realm of possibility.

If for some reason your ranges don't overlap, that means there's no deal to be had. If, for example, you have only $5 in your pocket and the pants vendor's costs are $7, he can't go any lower and you can't afford to go any higher. There's no agreement to be made unless

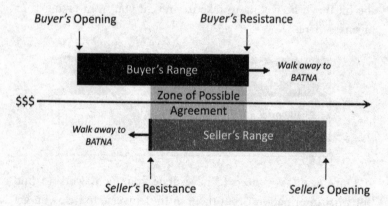

Figure 4: The zone of possible agreement (ZOPA) is the range in which both parties can agree to a deal. Anything outside of this zone is unacceptable to one party or the other.

circumstances change—either you find more cash or the vendor drops his price because he needs to liquidate his stock for whatever he can get. But if the circumstances aren't changing, there's no point in wasting time or energy on the negotiation.

WHERE'S THE FINISH LINE? YOUR TARGET

In a negotiation, it's always important to start with the end in mind. Otherwise you're guessing your way through the whole negotiation and getting to a suboptimal place. It's like saying, "I know I want to go to an amusement park, but I'll just figure out how to get there as I go." If you're not careful, you'll end up in a swamp in Florida instead of at Walt Disney World. You need to know where you're going if you're ever going to find a route to get there. In My Way negotiations, this is where the target comes into play. The target is where you want to finish the whole deal, the promised land where you've maxed out value. It's the ideal scenario.

Professional negotiators will tell you to err on the side of being aspirational instead of too realistic. Aim high and you're more likely to finish high. Studies show us time and again that those who have more aspirational targets get better results.[7]

At this point you're probably sick of all of these elements to prepare. But I have some good news for you: you've already done the work on this one because *your target* is *their resistance point*. Whaaat? That's right. This is the "me" side of the negotiation spectrum: whatever I take, you lose; and whatever you take, I lose. So, if you're going to maximize this deal, you want to leave nothing on the table. That also means that their least appealing option is your most appealing option (and vice versa).

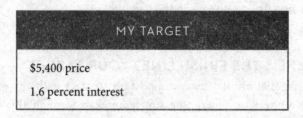

MY TARGET

$5,400 price

1.6 percent interest

Some people I speak to get uncomfortable with this concept because they feel bad about giving the other person a bad deal. Let's get this straight: this is their LEAST appealing option. It's still more appealing than going to their BATNA, or they would have gone there already. You're not trying to get them to agree to something that is outside of the realm of possibility or that's going to drive them into bankruptcy. There are even ways to make them feel quite satisfied about accepting their least appealing option—we'll get to that shortly. So, recall that this dark-side negotiation is all about looking out for your best interests—because the other party is not going to be doing it for you.

A reminder about your mindset: when you go into the negotiation, your resistance point should be all but a distant memory—it's locked away in that "in case of emergency" box. The number you want to have on your mind going into the negotiation is what they are capable of giving you: their resistance point is your target, and it's what should be taking up all of your mental focus. If you've ever driven a car, you know that you need to keep your eyes looking ahead at your target. If you start looking off to the left, your car is going to naturally start veering in that direction—and onto the shoulder or into the path of oncoming traffic. That spells disaster. The same is true when you negotiate. If you go in thinking about your worst-case scenario, you're going to start veering toward it. You need to make sure you keep your focus where you need it most. That means considering your worst-case scenario only in an emergency.

KEEP YOUR POWER WITH QUESTIONS

What happens if you're so out of your depth that your assumptions feel weak? What if you've just started your trek through Thailand and you haven't come across any other sellers yet, or these pants aren't exactly like the last ones you saw? What do you need to know, or what can you find out, about this seller and his product to make an educated decision? What kind of assumptions would you make about his options and BATNAs? What can you ask about the type of fabric or where the pants are made? Start with making some assumptions and test them out by making some statements in conversation to either confirm or deny them. Or ask a question to verify what you've suspected all along. Any bits of information you can gather can help you to test out those assumptions and feel more confident about those educated guesses.

Remember: knowledge is power. How can you get more of it? By asking questions. Consider what kind of questions you may need to have ready in case you get stuck and have over- or underestimated what's going on.

Don't try to use this last tip as an excuse to avoid filling out the other party's side of the preparation document (I've seen students do exactly that, and it drives me bananas). You need to at least take a stab at it by applying some common sense. Consider the scenario at the car dealership. Are you dealing with an individual seller you found online? Why do you think he or she is trying to sell? Did they drop any hints in their advertisement? Why aren't they going through a dealer or doing a trade-in? How long has the car been on the market? Are you the first person who has commented or reached out? What does that tell you about how much interest there is in that car, or how desperate the seller may be feeling to unload it?

You may want to craft some careful questions to get them to divulge some of these pressures. You may not be able to be direct, lest they get freaked out and shut down, but write down anything noteworthy and consider how you can work it into the conversation to suss out the situation. You could ask questions about their family to see if there are any young drivers in the house and how well the car was taken care of. Asking about when it was last painted will indicate whether there has been any damage (few people paint cars unprompted). Instead of asking what's wrong with it, you may want to ask if they'd mind if you took it to your mechanic to get it checked out. Then pause and see how they handle answering that one. If they protest, you may want to start probing deeper . . . or start looking for a different car.

If you feel like you're getting stuck and you don't want to make a concession, questions are also an effective way to access the pause button. Ask a question—even something you already know the answer to—to confirm what you know, to potentially get some additional information, or just to buy yourself time to think about what to do next while they answer. Of course, if you are asking a question you *don't* know the answer to, you'd better be damn sure to listen to what they're sharing. Doing a little listening still gives your brain a break from thinking. Asking a question is a great way to pause and get yourself to calm down and focus on them instead of on your nerves. I'm a big advocate of getting comfortable with silence and using that time to calm your mind. If your counterparts don't know how to handle silence, they may freak out and start giving you valuable information and clues. If they are comfortable with silence (and you're not), then asking them a question is a great way to get them talking and prevent yourself from giving away valuable information.

CHAPTER 18

PLANNING THE MOVES
(HOW DO WE GET THERE?)

YOU KNOW WHERE YOU WANT TO END UP, BUT HOW ARE you going to get there? It's time to nail the choreography to make sure you can get from point A to point B. After all, if you were going to take a road trip to Walt Disney World, you would have to plan out a route. When I was a kid, we made that exact road trip, and my dad relied on a giant book of maps to figure out how to get us all the way from Canada to Florida. I remember watching him trace the lines on the map and then, when we were in the car, I remember watching out for the signs that matched our next moves to get to Mickey. I loved the feeling that I was helping to navigate. I wonder which came first: my love for road trips or my love for negotiation? Chicken or egg?

When you're trying to get somewhere, you definitely don't want to be guessing your way there. You'll feel anxious, which means you'll start making mistakes, questioning your judgment, getting too distracted to check blind spots, feeling some road rage, lashing out at people . . . it's not pretty. You'll likely find yourself having to backtrack, and by the time you get to Disney World, it will probably be closed. Epic fail. The same is true in negotiation. Once you find yourself under pressure to make the next move, mistakes start to happen and it can lead to deadlock.

There's an easy way to avoid all of this frustration: Plan. Your. Moves.

You know where you want to finish, but where do you begin?

MAKE YOUR FIRST MOVES EXTREME

You know you want to finish at their resistance point (or as close as you can to it), but they're not going to just willingly go to their least satisfying option and declare, "Please, feel free to take all of my extra money." This is where the dance of satisfaction comes back into play. Those rituals I mentioned earlier are important tools to manage the other party's satisfaction. The move plan we discussed is an integral part of this dance. Knowing where you want to finish is half the battle. It's your reference point for figuring out where to start.

If you start exactly where you want to finish, they'll respond in one of two ways: "No way in hell," or "Okay."

If they answer, "No way in hell," then:

1. You stay at that exact spot without moving, because you don't want to give up any of that target value you're chasing. In time, they get frustrated, and one or both of you will walk away in frustration, with or without a deal.

This happens because people expect these rituals, and so the other party assumes that you have
some moves left and they start the dance. They make
another proposal, assuming you've got more proposals left in you, to get closer to their favorable side of
the zone of possible agreement (ZOPA). When you
don't dance with them, they get pissed off, even if
they're getting a great deal.

2. Or, you start making concessions, fumbling your
way through the ZOPA until you finally reach some
compromise, which means you don't capture the
maximum value you were trying to achieve.

If you ever have to deal with them again, they now
have the expectation that you are a generous negotiator, and if you gave them such a great deal this time,
they're going to push a little harder to get an even
better deal next time.

If they say, "Okay," you may be relieved and think, "That was easy."
And then you think, "Wait . . . that was *too* easy. How much did I
just leave on the table?" Odds are, you under- or overestimated their
resistance point, and the other party, knowing they're getting a steal
of a deal, are trying to get out of there before you can back out! Even
if you got what was objectively the bargain of the century, you're
probably feeling unsatisfied because your instincts tell you there was
opportunity for more, simply because it was too. Damn. Easy.

When it comes to satisfaction, if you're starting at the target,
it's all downhill. Negotiations that go too easily can also leave you

doubting the value of what you've just acquired and make you ask yourself whether you really want it. If you close a deal without doing the dance with the other party, they're going to assume something's wrong because you've made it too easy for them. Imagine you're house-hunting, and you find one with an asking price of $700,000. If you offer them $600,000 and they agree right away, what would you be thinking? Probably something along the lines of "Uh-oh, what the hell is wrong with this house? Why did they sell it to me so quickly? Why wasn't anyone else trying to buy it? Does it have termites? Asbestos? The world's worst neighbors?" You can drive yourself crazy wondering about all of the terrible things that could be wrong with this house . . . all because the seller didn't dance with you.

But if they resisted your offer and countered with an offer a lot closer to their list price—say, $685,000—and then after a few more back-and-forth offers you finally settled on a price of $658,000, how do you think you'd be feeling? You'd be bragging to all of your friends and family that you, the master negotiator, had managed to get the sellers to drop their price by $42,000—a formidable feat. A dance to be admired. It's nothing compared to the $100,000 reduction you achieved in the first example, but you're not coming away from this one full of doubt. It feels so good. Go you! Whereas in the first example, you probably would have been on the phone immediately with a home inspector—and possibly a lawyer to figure out how the hell to get out of this deal.

These are two very different levels of satisfaction. And the difference has everything to do with the way you handled the dance— and *nothing* to do with the final negotiated price!

The key element to starting the journey to satisfaction is the opening offer. On the dark side, when we're talking about "me" negotiations, it's appropriate to dance with some bigger steps with what is called an *extreme opener*. In this scenario, you know their resistance point and you pick an opening figure well outside of the ZOPA. Why? Because they're expecting you to dance. Now, you may ask, "How extreme is extreme?" That's not an easy one to answer. There's no magic formula. You're going to have to use some gut instincts and common sense. But here is one guideline that will help: the farther over you are on the dark side of the spectrum—no relationship, a one-time transaction, no further contact—the more extreme you can afford to go.

Bear in mind, you don't want to go so extreme that they laugh you out of the room. Imagine going to the elephant pants vendor and saying, "I want them for free," or "I'll give you one dollar." That would be so insulting that they probably wouldn't even step onto the dance floor with you. But an offer of $5 might not seem quite as ridiculous to them.

If you're starting from such an extreme position that your next move is to double your offer, that might not seem so credible. Imagine offering $300,000 for that house and then jumping to $600,000 in the next breath. If the seller wasn't completely insulted that you started so low, they'd assume that you must have another big jump in you. Either way, not a good expectation for you to have to manage.

How extreme you go will depend on some common sense and intuition, but here are a couple of guiding principles to bear in mind:

- Make sure the offer is outside of the ZOPA (otherwise, it's not extreme and won't deliver satisfaction).
- And, the farther you move toward the lighter side of the spectrum, the less extreme you go.

Satisfaction is always a priority, but how you deliver it changes slightly as you glide along the spectrum. As you start to develop trust, because you have to deal with the other party again, your extremes become a little less extreme. Let's say you are dealing with a salary negotiation, which generally falls somewhere in the middle of the spectrum. If you started out by demanding $100,000, even though you had it on good authority that the highest they could go was $65,000, then your extreme would be ridiculous. Perhaps $78,000 would be a bit more appropriate in this case. You have to decide on a case-by-case basis, asking yourself, "Does this offer or demand pass the credibility test? Would I be annoyed at someone who came into the negotiation this extreme?" Your gut instinct should be able to give you a decent answer to get you on your way. If not, run it by someone else. You are pausing to prepare anyway, so you should build in a moment to do that as part of your research.

The other reason why opening extreme is so valuable is that it helps take some of the guesswork out of gauging the other party's resistance point. Since guessing is not a science (and not foolproof), sometimes we can get it wrong. Fortunately, opening outside of what we *think* is the ZOPA gives us a chance to test our theory and redeem ourselves if necessary.

Let's say you're on the beach, ready to buy your pants, and you have guessed that the seller's resistance point is $15. You've decided to open extreme at $10, but you don't get any protest from the seller. He may not be agreeing with you, ready to hand over the goods, but you also haven't heard a no—or any reaction, for that matter. He seems to be considering it. Uh-oh. You must be hovering around the edge of the ZOPA. You've overestimated his resistance and you were about to leave money on the table by trying to finish at $15. Good thing you tested that resistance point. Now you've got a last chance to improve your negotiation and save yourself some money by hanging out at $10 a little longer, or perhaps moving only slightly, to $11, to close a deal. Had you opened at or close to $15, you might as well have been handing over your wallet.

REMEMBER THE DANCE OF SATISFACTION

Some of you may be wondering why I didn't just tell you to slam on the brakes at $10 and never move again. While that's not impossible, it's not going to deliver much satisfaction to the seller. If you open at a number and just stay there without moving, you're not dancing. And we are wired to expect a dance in these circumstances. Our experience and intuition tell us there's room for movement, so when we don't get any, we get frustrated. Some may get so frustrated that they refuse to close the deal with you, even if it means they're missing out on a great opportunity! Huh?! Remember, we're not always rational, we're human, and our egos get in the way. Causing someone frustration, especially someone who doesn't know how to access their inner pause button, can cause all sorts of kooky reactions. The best way to relieve that frustration and bring them some satisfaction is by completing the ritual and making a move—even if it's just a tiny one. So, moving from $10 to $11 will send a message that you're trying to dance, but you have limited funds, so they should be satisfied with what little you are bringing. You'll get a much better response from that move than starting at $15 and never budging from there. Seriously: giving them $4 less, but taking that extra step to do it, will make them more satisfied than not moving on the dance floor with them. People. Are. Crazy. It gives them an ego boost if they can say, "Ah, yes, she moved, just as I predicted," instead of "Why isn't this crazy [woman] playing along with me?"

This isn't something that we need to be taught, as evidenced by children who do it intuitively. If you don't believe me, start spending some time with kids; I guarantee you're going to see them opening extreme all over the place. Supermodel Chrissy Teigen posted a video of her three-year old daughter, Luna, negotiating the "candy trials" on June 3, 2019 (which I've reposted on my Instagram account, @fotiniicon). In traditional negotiating fashion, here's how it went down:

> **Chrissy:** How many pieces of candy? I say one. What do you say?
> **Luna:** I say [*holds up three fingers*].
> **Chrissy:** What about one?
> **Luna:** No, I want three.
> **Chrissy:** What about two?
> **Luna:** Yes. [*Cue the applause.*]

You'll notice that when Chrissy repeated her initial offer of one, Luna mirrored her behavior and did the same, holding at her proposal of three. *But*, when Mommy made a move, Luna mirrored her there too and decided to meet her at two. This is how the dance is done—in this case, with no instruction given, just human nature doing its thing.

We can take that same knowledge of human nature and apply it to our move plans. Opening extreme is the first step in leaving space on the dance floor to make some moves and test your assumptions about where you think your counterpart's resistance point may be.

THE NEXT MOVES

We've determined the target and the opening move, but you don't want to be aimlessly guessing your way to the target. You need to plan out the rest of your moves too. Let's go back to our car example. If you have anticipated the seller's resistance point to be $5,400, you might decide to open extreme at $4,300. If you're like me, and like to use paper, you'd jot that on your planning document.

My opening move: $4,300

My next moves:

$ _____

$ _____

$ _____

$ _____

My target: $5,400

(As a side note, studies show that we remember things better when we physically write them down—that's why I encourage my students to write notes instead of typing them. The advantage in a negotiation is that you can always bring that scrap of paper with you instead of trying to remember all of this information in your head. That document becomes a physical manifestation of the pause button that you can look at to trigger your memory and rational thought when you get overwhelmed or frustrated.)

When you plug your current location and your destination into Google Maps, it spits out the optimal route and tells you which turns to make to get to where you want to go. We want to decide those turns now as well. Now, I know you're going to cry out, "But I don't know what they're going to say in the negotiation, so how can I possibly know how I'm going to respond?" Well, Google Maps can't predict with 100 percent accuracy what's going to be happening when you get on the road, and when it needs to, it will reroute, using all of the data it has at its disposal. And as I showed in the example with overestimating the other party's $15 resistance point, you can do the same. But most of the time, just like on the map, people and moves are predictable. Remember that your behavior affects the other party's behavior to a huge degree. Just as when Luna's mom made a move, she was compelled to follow suit, they will respond to your move plans, and you're likely to end up pretty close to where you anticipated.

If talks aren't going according to plan, look at your map (hopefully you brought that paper planning note in with you) and press pause to reroute. Just like Google Maps, you have the option to readjust in real time, but unless there's a major obstacle in the way, why would you? And if you spot a more efficient or more profitable route, as in the $11 example I gave above, go for it! Seize the opportunity. Your foresight and pause button have given you the capacity to find a better way to get there. Planning nothing will leave you fumbling, causing frustration for both sides, and you're less likely to finish the dance by hitting your target (or anything close to it).

So, what should the moves look like between your opener and your target? A pattern. But not just any pattern. With those pants on the beach, you could open at $4, and then move to $6, then $8, and finally $10. Do you spot a pattern? So did the other guy. If he sees you going up in increments of $2, guess what his expectations are going to be when you get to $10? He'll sit back and assume you've got at least another $2 in you, if not a few more multiples of two. He definitely won't feel compelled to stop dancing at $10. You've managed his expectations to keep the dance going in the hope that you keep shelling out these $2 increments. And what do you think will happen when you abruptly stop at $10 because you don't want to overshoot your target? Frustration it is. You'll be tripping the ego wire, and good luck trying to close this deal without him cursing at you on the way out.

How about this one? You start at $4, move to $7, then to $8, then to $10. Pattern? Big, small, big . . . what would you anticipate next? Maybe another big jump, maybe not, but the other party will probably expect *something*, because it doesn't feel like you're done. The seller still anticipates that there's something more coming after $10, so he won't want to meet you there to close the deal.

I should mention that all of these moves are in response to something that the other party has offered. You're not sitting there negotiating against yourself while the other party stays silent (though I have seen that happen plenty of times, and it leaves me shaking my head). You're putting an offer out there, pausing to wait for their response, pausing to react to their response (or letting them sweat it out), making your next move, and so on. So, the dialogue could look like this:

> **You:** I'll give you $4.
> **Seller:** [*Assuming this wasn't so insulting he's walking away.*]
> Are you kidding?! I need $20 for these pants.
> **You:** I'll give you $7.
> **Seller:** No, no, no. I can do $16.
> **You:** Eight.
> **Seller:** I can give them to you for $14.
> **You:** Will you take $10?
> **Seller:** No. I need more than that.

There's some frustration brewing. The pattern might have triggered his Spidey sense (deep in his subconscious) that there is more money to be made, and he's hesitant to make another move, urging you to offer up what you've got in your pocket. If you try to end it now, there's going to be no satisfaction and possibly no deal. But what if we tried one more pattern?

> **You:** I'll give you $4.
> **Seller:** Are you kidding?! I need $20 for these pants.
> **You:** I'll give you $7.
> **Seller:** No, no, no. I can do $16.

So far, everything is going okay. You've moved and he's made an even bigger move.

You: I can do $9.

This move is slightly smaller than your last one, and he will sense that you're both making progress.

Seller: I will sell them for $13.
You: I've got $10 for them.
Seller: Okay, I'll take $10.

This is a likely scenario, because your moves have gone from $4 to $7 to $9 to $10. This pattern of decreasing size is a signal to the subconscious that we're coming to an end and running out of offers. If the other party sees this as a credible end to the pattern (some of which has to do with the language and delivery we'll discuss later), he is more compelled to make even bigger moves than you did to meet you at that desired end point. If you're still truly outside of his ZOPA, he'll at least keep going as far as he can, and you can have a small backup move that won't spoil the pattern and mismanage his expectations. If he had come down to $12 or $11, it wouldn't be out of line for you to inch a little bit closer with one more dollar.

The key is to make sure the pattern isn't erratic or getting bigger. Moves of decreasing size will signal that you are nearing the end of your proposals, and thus the negotiation, so he needs to get on board if the offer is within his ZOPA.

I know you're thinking this sounds silly, and if it's so easy, won't the other party see right through it? Maybe. Probably. But it's the dance we've come to expect, and we feel satisfied with the choreography as long as the pattern sits well with our psychology. It's the same way that the person who asked, "Hi, how are you" doesn't expect you to share all of your latest trials and tribulations; instead, you reply with the choreographed "Fine, thanks." We both know that it's all part of the routine, but we settle into this ritual naturally and feel a sense of satisfaction for having participated in it.

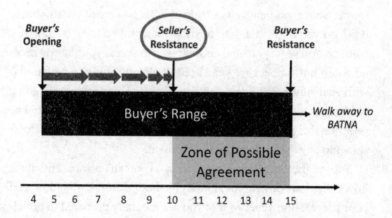

Figure 5: Plan your moves in ever-decreasing sizes as you get closer to their resistance point.

ANTICIPATING HOW THEY'RE GOING TO MOVE: THEIR OPENER

One of the easiest ways to brace yourself for whatever is to come is to anticipate the other side's extreme opener as well. Take a moment to fill out another spot on the preparation document: their opening move.

Recall that we're on the dark "me" side of negotiation, and your target is their worst-case scenario. Unsurprisingly, their target is your worst-case scenario. They're going to try to push you as far as you can go, and the best way they can do that is by opening extreme—outside the ZOPA. So, you can easily anticipate that they're going to open well outside of what you're willing or able to do. And you'll avoid a case of sticker shock because you saw this coming. You've just created another way to access your handy mental pause button because your brain is already going to be familiar with that number. It's the one you expected and knew was going to be an absurd proposal. They know, and *you* know, that you'll be rejecting this proposal. You just need to pause to remember why it's showing up when you get in the moment.

You might get the number wrong—you can't always anticipate how ridiculous or extreme they'll go—but put something down on your preparation sheet so that you are mentally prepared to anticipate that some sort of ridiculous number is going to come up. That way, there's no reason to lose your cool when that moment comes—pause button accessed once again! When you're at the car dealership and you see or hear a number like $11,000, you press pause, swat that number away and focus on your move plan that will get you closer to *your* target.

> **Their opening move: $11,000**

Then what?

There's one thing you should do before you move back to your plan and counter-propose: react. If you say nothing, with a stoic look on your face, they will have no idea that their proposal was unacceptable or extreme. Remember that one of the reasons we open extreme is to determine whether we guessed the ZOPA and their resistance point correctly. If you're not giving them any indication that their proposal was in walk-away territory, they'll have to assume by default that they are in, or close to, the ZOPA and they'll hesitate to keep moving toward your target. They'll try to hang out at the more favorable end of the ZOPA in an attempt to maximize the deal.

Let's say your six-year-old is on the way out the door in his Superman cape, and when you ask where he's going, he says, "I'm just going to climb up the tree to practice my flying." If you say nothing, then why should he change his trajectory in any way? He'll stay on plan, keep marching out the door and start climbing his way to his next broken bone. If, however, you say something appropriately as extreme in your response—like "WHAT?!" or "No, you are NOT!"—he will be jolted into changing course, or at least pausing to discuss some sort of compromise with you. Your response, whether audible or just a look of shock and/or dismay, will likely have to be as extreme as the initial flying proposal was in the first place.

The same is true of your negotiations. If you say nothing when they come out with some ridiculous extreme—perhaps one that was even more extreme than you anticipated in your preparation—you need to have some reaction ready to knock them off course and get them back in line with yours. Acting as though you're cool with $12,000, $8,000 or even $6,000 (either by saying nothing or saying something positive about it) won't get them close to your $5,400 target. The only time you need to indicate you're cool with the proposal is when they've approached your target. A raise of the eyebrows, drop of the jaw, shake of the head or audible gasp can work wonders at a car dealership.

WHY SPLITTING THE DIFFERENCE GETS YOU A BAD DEAL

The majority of the MBA students I teach are international students, and they share some fun and interesting stories with me, both in class and in their final papers, where they identify some of their mistakes and recall success stories. A bunch of my students come from India to study, and as a result, I've often heard a phrase come up in their negotiations once each side has made a proposal: "Okay, *neither mine nor yours*, let's split the difference, you can take this item at 350 rupees."

"Neither mine nor yours" is a line frequently used by street vendors at Colaba Causeway, one of the most famous jewelry/trinket streets in Mumbai. Market vendors in areas like this have a reputation for being experienced negotiators, and my students, like many others, fall prey to this line (a literal translation of the Hindi colloquialism *na mera na aapka*), which is equivalent to the English phrase "let's split the difference." Ask yourself: why would somebody be willing to compromise so easily, to abandon both their last proposal and yours and split the difference by meeting you in the middle (or somewhere close to it)? I can assure you that in a "me" negotiation, it's not out of the goodness of their hearts. Let's explore the ZOPA for this situation and consider what happens when one party opens way more extreme than the other.

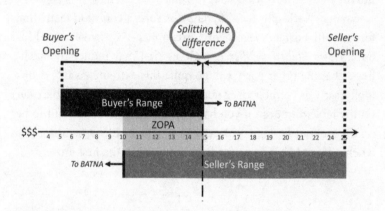

Figure 6: Who benefits from splitting the difference? The person whose starting point was more extreme.

In the example shown above, if the buyer opens at $5 and the seller opens at $25, the difference is $20. Thus, splitting the difference would mean settling for $15, with the two sides meeting each other $10 away from their opening position. This sounds quite fair, right? Wrong. The seller has opened so much more extreme than the buyer that splitting the difference means capturing all of the value in the ZOPA and pushing the buyer to their resistance point.

The buyer may not even notice they're getting a bad deal because it *seems* so fair to split things. But if you don't know the size of the pie, how do you know how to split it? Phrases like "let's split the difference" or "neither mine nor yours" should set off alarm bells to the negotiator who is listening carefully. It's a signal that the other party has opened extreme, so of course they are willing to cut a deal—it's heavily in their favor to do so.

Saying, "Let's split the difference" is such a common tactic that former FBI hostage negotiator Christopher Voss even named his book *Never Split the Difference*. Going first may reduce the likelihood that the other party will go quite this extreme, as they won't look nearly as credible once you've put your more reasonable offer on the table. But even if you have gone first, you'll still want to be on the lookout for tactics like this one. (The next chapter discusses when it is, and isn't, to your advantage to make the first move.)

CHAPTER 19

WHO'S ON FIRST?

ONE OF THE AGE-OLD QUESTIONS IN NEGOTIATION INVOLVES who should communicate their proposal first. Some say the seller should go first, while others say the buyer should make the first move. Some say you should make the other party go first, and others say you should be the one to make the first move. I could stay on the fence and tell you it depends, but I'm not going to do that to you. I may not have strong feelings about who should make the first move in the dating world, but I do have a strong opinion in the negotiating world. Before I tell you what that is, let's explore some different negotiating situations.

If you step onto a used car lot, you're inevitably going to see some big stickers or signs on cars with prices on them. When you are approached by the guy on the beach selling the elephant pants, you probably don't even have a chance to ask, "How much?" before they tell you about the special price they've set just for you. Job listings often mention a salary or a range. Even at many auctions, whether silent auctions or the eBay variety, it's unusual not to see a minimum bid or estimated value in the description. When this happens, your subconscious picks up on these details and manages your expectations about the end point for the negotiation.

Those messages can be more powerful that you realize. Imagine you've done your homework on the book value for a particular used car—you've looked up sales data and everything—and you expect it to be priced at $5,500. You walk onto the lot and you are shocked to see a sticker in the window that says $9,500. They don't call it sticker shock for nothing! Your brain goes into overdrive and you begin to doubt the research you did: maybe you didn't dig deep enough; maybe this one has some added features the others don't have; maybe the dealer knows something you don't. Or maybe you're like me and you think, "How dare they try to rip me off? They don't know who they're dealing with!" as you brace for battle to take them down, confident in your research (or is that just me?).

The point is that they've managed your expectations. You can succumb to the sticker shock, or you can press your pause button to recall that you know what you're doing and you prepared for this. You've got this! It's hard to do, but you stand a much better chance of resisting this influence if you've done your homework.

If you've ever been in a negotiation over a job offer, you might have heard the question most of my students dread most: "What are your salary expectations?" I sort of understand where the dread comes from. It's the fear of the employer saying, "How dare you ask for that much? You're so out of line, I'm rescinding the offer!" Occasionally, some students fear going too low and undercutting themselves. One of the best ways to manage the risk of any of that happening is just to do your homework. Just as you would look up the recent sale prices of the model of car you're looking for or of houses in the neighborhood you want to buy into, you would come into this negotiation with an educated assessment of what the employer should be paying for *you*. Then you'll decide on an appropriately extreme or aspirational opener and a target move plan. Here's what happens when you answer that question and put your proposal down first (after you've prepared, of course): you set the stage for where this negotiation will end. Will it end closer to your aspirational opener, or to their lowball offer?

What happens when the average untrained or uncontrolled negotiator gets sticker shock? Panic sets in and they think, "Oh no! How am I going to drag them away from that unanticipated $9,500 figure?" They start spinning their wheels, thinking about that unexpected number. Their subconscious gets preoccupied with this number instead of the one it should be focused on: their own target. If they haven't prepared the way you have (or *will*, for every negotiation you ever do from now on, for the rest of eternity), they don't even have a target to redirect their brain to. Double trouble. So now, not only are they focused on this number that's dragging them away from their target, but they also don't have the means to latch onto a number that's going to be more favorable to them.

Imagine going into a car dealership and thinking, "Wow, that $9,500 was much more than I expected. I wonder if I can get it for less than $9,500. I wonder how much lower they'd be willing to go than $9,500." How many times has your brain registered the number 9,500? When you're driving, which direction should your eyes be looking? In the direction that you're headed. If you start looking elsewhere, that's where you'll end up. If your brain is focused on the number $9,500, which direction is it headed? Which figure is it trying to get more comfortable with? You guessed it: $9,500. And which number *should* you be focused on in a negotiation? Your *target*, otherwise known as *their resistance point*. But they managed to distract your focus with their silly sticker. Their first proposal has been made, and you haven't even made contact with them yet!

Let's try this again with the elephant pants. The seller tells the buyer, "I'll give them to you for the special price of $25." The buyer starts thinking, "Damn, I was going to offer $5, but now that he's said they're $25, I don't want to seem like a real jerk compared to his price. Maybe I should increase my opening offer to $10." Mission accomplished (for the seller). He just got you to make a move before you even opened your mouth. Of course, this was all the more effective because that first move was also rather extreme.

Let's leave the beach and revisit that salary negotiation. It could go a different way. Instead of giving you the opening to go first and asking you your salary expectations, it's just as common for an interviewer to make you an offer without those expectations. In this case, perhaps you've been expecting the offer to be better than what you're currently making, especially since you know you've been underpaid for your experience level and you know what the rest of the market is offering. Instead, it comes in lower. You're shocked, then disappointed, then doubtful of what you are worth. Maybe *they* didn't get it wrong; maybe *you* did, and you've been overvaluing yourself the whole time! That fear-and-doubt game is strong.

Your pause button feels so far out of reach. You're scrambling to figure out how you'll even convince them to pay you your current salary, let alone how much more you were aspiring to earn.

You'd just be grateful to have a few thousand more than what they're offering, so I guess that's your new target, right? Wrong. Because you've read this book (and this section specifically), you're going to take a deep breath to access that pause button and go back to your preparation. But that's hard to do. Because this compensation discussion is a little farther into the gray zone (assuming you are talking about a role you want to stay in for more than a few weeks or months), we're going to go over how to prepare for a salary negotiation in a little more depth in a later section, but you get the gist of what's going on here.

ANCHORING: THE BENEFITS OF GOING FIRST

There is a benefit in going first. In each of these scenarios, the other party has managed to throw you off, rattle your confidence, create some doubt and get you to hit the panic button instead of the pause button. In negotiation research, stating a number first is called *anchoring*.

On a recent sailing trip, whenever we weren't on the move, we were usually docked at a marina with ropes tied to the dock to keep us in place. However, we spent one night floating at sea. Our host assured us we wouldn't drift away and crash into any other boats because we would drop an anchor, which would keep us from moving very far. Once that anchor dropped, we would move only as far as the chain attached to it could reach. In negotiation, the party who goes first is dropping that anchor, making it difficult for the other to drag them away from that spot. It would take some serious strength to do so.

A well-prepared negotiator can overcome this obstacle. They just need to reach their mental pause button and focus on their target, instead of allowing themselves to get dragged by the anchor to the other person's target. If you hear them go first, just redirect your focus right back to the data from your preparation—it hasn't changed just because they anchored. You're not going to let them influence you. You go back to your opening offer and use it as a counter to their initial offer. Tell them what they're going to have to do to get to a deal. Whether it's in the form of a first offer or a first counteroffer, you can get to the same target as long as you keep your focus on your target. Press pause to take a breath, minimize their influence and get back on your plan.

WHEN IT'S BETTER NOT TO ANCHOR

Whenever I talk about this subject in a workshop, I pose the question of who should go first to my students and clients. Inevitably, at least one person (usually more) answers that you should force the other party to go first because they'll give away clues about their position and potentially their resistance point. Here's the issue with that response: most of the time, you know enough about the situation at hand, whether you're buying those pants, a car, or anything else that's within Google's reach, to make an educated guess about resistance points and targets. That means they're not giving you anything that's totally foreign to you; you've likely already anticipated all of the information they might divulge. If you've followed the instructions found here so far, they're just confirming your preparation. Study after study, and even my own experiments in my classrooms, indicate that the one who goes first gets the better deal. I have yet to see any compelling evidence to the contrary.

The only reasons I've ever found compelling enough to want the other party to go first are:

- You are totally clueless about the negotiation subject matter, to the point where there is no history to look up and you know *no one*, not even Siri or Google, who can give you an indicator of where this could go.
- Or, you are so unbelievably nervous that you think you'll fumble it so badly that you're going to hurt your own credibility.

You'd have to work extremely hard to show me an instance where the first of these scenarios is true; I find it hard to believe that you'll go into any unprecedented negotiation without at least some indicators of what success would look like. Seriously, try me: if you can think of them, I'd like to have some examples to share with my audiences. The only ones I have are so obscure that they're not worth spending time discussing here.

As for the second scenario, my hope for you is that in reading this book you will be able to find the courage, confidence and mindset to find a way to access your pause button and pull yourself together to go for what you deserve. You've made it this far; what's holding you back? Why wouldn't you try to give yourself every possible advantage to get what you want?

CHAPTER 20

BEFORE YOU AGREE

WHAT IF THEIR FIRST OFFER IS REALLY, *REALLY* GOOD? Then, my friend, you've underestimated their resistance point, and the ZOPA is bigger than you anticipated. The temptation will be to take the offer and pop the champagne. DON'T DO IT! Press pause, keep your cool and rejig your plan to get them to make another concession. Trust me: they've got the room to do it. If you rush to pour the champagne and it seems too easy, they're going to be wondering what's wrong with this deal. Remember the example of the house purchase in chapter 18? The one where the negotiations were too easy, threatening to keep you up all night worrying about the possibility of termites in this potential money pit you've bought? The same principle applies here: the other party will be wondering why you accepted their offer so quickly. You don't want them (or you) to end up walking away with regrets, so do them a favor and get them to make another concession by making a counterproposal. Twisted and weird, huh? Welcome back to the psychology we discussed earlier. People. Are. Crazy.

I've heard some clients tell me that they don't care if the other party has regrets as long as they themselves got a great deal. "What do I care what the other guy thinks if this is all about me anyway?" I don't blame you for thinking this, but it does take two to tango. If they have regrets, there's a chance they might pull the plug on this negotiation—perhaps even seconds after you've walked away. A canceled payment, a bad review or ill will can all lead to costly repercussions you could easily avoid if you just give the other party a little satisfaction. It costs you nothing and, as described earlier, it could actually make you richer to deliver some satisfaction to the other person.

We can see that, contrary to popular belief, satisfaction doesn't come from giving them everything they want. Sometimes it comes from holding back and playing hard to get. Next time you hang out with a kid like Luna, give them all the candy they were asking for. You might be thinking, "She only asked for three? I would have given her four!" Give her the three and within minutes, if not seconds, she'll be asking for four, then five—and the next time she might start at ten! The kid will want more candy than she can possibly consume (spend any time around children at Halloween and tell me that's not true). She'll never be satisfied. All because she never got any resistance. Not even a moment's hesitation.

Sometimes that's all you need. If you want her to have the three pieces of candy, no judgment here. But if you're contemplating how to make sure you don't set a precedent, consider how you can show a little resistance. You don't even have to counter-propose, but before you agree, just hit the pause button. Take a breath. Sigh audibly or say, "Hmmm . . . let me think about it." Make it look like you're contemplating it, let her sweat it out for a few extra seconds, and you'll build up the anticipation that increases her satisfaction. Temper tantrum and greed-monster crisis averted for another day. Sometimes, you just need to slow it down to create some efficiencies.

I recall working with a former union leader who had some entertaining stories to tell. Most of the time, negotiations are actually quite dull, like watching paint dry, but occasionally they can get dramatic, and union–management negotiations are the ones that usually draw out those cinematic moments. If you've ever read a press release issued during teachers' union or autoworkers' union negotiations, they usually mention that "negotiators were working well into the night" and that "an agreement was reached just as the clock struck the midnight deadline." *Phew!* Both parties must have worked really hard to get everything they could out of that situation, using every minute they could to attempt to extract value, right? Those management and union reps must have done everything they possibly could, so both sides should be happy with the results!

This union leader told me that one of the deals he worked on was extremely basic, but the two sides couldn't afford to let anyone else know that. So, they took an extended break before they made the announcement that they had reached an agreement. "Can you imagine if we told the union we got it done so quickly?" he said. "We'd be crucified! It wouldn't have mattered that we got a fantastic deal, one that there was no way to improve; if they didn't think we were in there duking it out, they would think that the deal was garbage."

When I was in my early twenties, I had a car accident I was lucky to walk away from with few injuries, but I did have to be off work for six months due to some severe whiplash. Without boring you with all of the details, I ended up with an experienced personal injury lawyer and we went through mediation with the other driver's insurance company. After I answered a bunch of questions the lawyers and mediators asked, the other party's lawyer made us an offer. I followed my lawyer out of the room to discuss the offer in private. We walked into a conference room, and after he shut the door, he told me, "This is an excellent offer. You're not going to do better than that, but we're going to hang out in here for a while and make them think I'm trying to convince you to take it, so just sit tight while I call my secretary to catch up on some other work."

(Before you assume I won the car-accident lottery, it wasn't life-changing, but after the fees, it was just enough to reimburse me for the income I lost—which was the target.) It was my first formal lesson in negotiation satisfaction. I'm not suggesting you start concocting ridiculous plans to dupe the other party, but consider how that little bit of hesitation can be another piece of choreography in the dance of satisfaction.

PAUSE FOR REFLECTION

SECTION 4 | THE PROCESS MY WAY:
THE COMPETITIVE SIDE
CHECKLIST OF KEY TAKEAWAYS

- ✓ **Satisfaction is the objective.** A little extra effort creates a lot of satisfaction and minimum resistance—prepare to do the dance to get maximum results.
- ✓ **Prepare!** Use a preparation document to help you nail your negotiation.
- ✓ **Identify your needs, then theirs.** If price is the primary focus for both of you—or even just one of you—then keep preparing for a "me" negotiation.
- ✓ **Identify resistance points.** Your resistance point is your "in case of emergency" move, and you need to keep it a secret. Their resistance point is your primary focus—it's your target!
- ✓ **Plan your moves.** Have a move plan, open extreme outside of the ZOPA, and make moves of decreasing size (without negotiating against yourself). Build in questions in case you get stuck.

✓ **Consider their moves.** Anticipate their opening move and be prepared to react.

✓ **Anchor.** Go first and take it slow.

✓ **Know your target.** Aim to finish at their resistance point, not yours.

✓ **Pause before agreeing.** Make sure you're maximizing the deal and that they feel satisfied.

SECTION 5

THE PROCESS OUR WAY:
THE COLLABORATIVE SIDE

CHAPTER 21

WHAT ARE WE AFTER? INTERESTS

AS ON THE DARK SIDE OF THE SPECTRUM, BOTH PARTIES come into a negotiation process on the lighter side with a set of objectives they want to achieve. On the "me" side, they're generally all tangible and/or quantitative interests, centering primarily on price or cost. As we move along the spectrum, price may or may not be what's driving the negotiation; rather, value is the name of the game, and value comes in forms that are both tangible and intangible. Security, time, safety, longevity, comfort, stress and good health are intangibles that can be more important than cash. What we learned on the dark side doesn't go out the window. We're just layering on some complexity and juggling a few extra balls in the process.

DEFINING MY ISSUES
As before, you start by defining your interests in the negotiation. What are your goals, and why are they important? Along with tangible factors like money, what intangible factors do you need to

consider? To illustrate a more complex negotiation, I'll walk you through a friend's decision-making process.

In Canada, we have a publicly funded basic healthcare system. That means that every Canadian has access to hospitals and physicians. It's not a perfect system, but it means no one is going bankrupt after having life-saving surgery. While there can be lengthy wait times for some non-urgent procedures, I've seen firsthand how effective our system can be. Over a decade ago my father had a triple bypass surgery to save him from a heart attack within days of diagnosis. Every day we have had together since that surgery has been a gift, and for that I am forever grateful to the wonderful doctors and the system that saved his life.

Though my father was fortunate to get immediate care for his life-threatening heart problem, Canadians waiting to see specialists like neurosurgeons and orthopedic surgeons are waiting a long time. And it's not because there aren't trained doctors waiting to see them. According to 2019 data from the Royal College of Physicians and Surgeons of Canada, the organization that oversees the medical education of specialists, nearly one in five newly certified specialists can't find a full-time job in Canada! One of the major reasons is that there isn't enough (public) funding for operating-room times and other resources that are needed to support these specialists. People like my dad, deemed on the brink of death, are going to be prioritized for that limited operating-room time over someone who needs knee-replacement surgery. That's not to say that knee surgery isn't medically necessary; it just means that the patient can afford to wait longer than my dad, so the patient and the surgeon are twiddling their thumbs until there's an operating-room slot and/or money to pay the surgeon to perform the operation. Until then, these surgeons are waiting for those who are already in practice to retire so that they can pick up the scalpel and take over, receiving what limited resources are available in the system.

For some newly trained specialists, it's not all bleak. While it may be difficult to find jobs in highly coveted urban centers like the Greater Toronto Area, there may be prospects in remote areas. One friend from my undergraduate days, Paulina, spent three years getting her bachelor's degree, followed by four years of medical school, plus a five-year residency in her surgical specialty, and finally two years studying a sub-specialty in her field. That's fourteen years of working her butt off and constantly finishing at the top of her class, only to find that that there were no options for her anywhere at all close to home. Paulina could wait around until someone retired in her preferred medical centers or consider options farther away— much farther away. When she investigated her opportunities away from home, she ended up with a few options. She narrowed these down to the only Canadian option and an opportunity in the US. Each was a three-hour flight from Toronto. One was in a remote city in northern Canada; the other was in the American South. She flew to both cities to explore the options in greater detail. Moving to the US would require her to take all sorts of certification exams and jump through immigration hoops, whereas the Canadian option would require no extra work—just getting used to a new place and a ridiculously cold winter.

Turns out, as accustomed as she was to winter in Toronto, northern Canada is a whole other level of cold. I mean walk-outside-and-your-nose-hairs-freeze-instantly kinda cold—on a daily basis! I am not cut out for such conditions. My friend isn't either. She decided that, as much as she would have loved to stay in Canada, the quality of life in the great white north, and of a life spent waiting around for her local predecessors to move on, just wasn't enough to make her stay. No salary was high enough to persuade her to make those sacrifices, especially after she had already spent fourteen years working and studying around the clock, waiting to finally settle into a lifestyle that would allow her to start enjoying some downtime. The hospital up north had even tried to offer a lot more vacation time than she would have received if she'd stayed closer to home. That would have allowed her to leave for long weekends on a regular basis to escape the cold and visit her friends and family back home. Still not enough.

The intangible value of being able to create a local support network and being able to walk around outside without freezing her butt off were just too damn important. And so . . . Paulina headed south of the border and, years later, hasn't looked back. Of course, the added value in that scenario was that I got a convenient guest room in a tropical climate at my disposal. Even though it didn't factor into her decision at all, that's an intangible I could get behind because I, too, truly hate winter.

As well as it all turned out for Paulina (and for me!), it wasn't an easy decision to make and it would have been torturous had she not been able to sort through her interests in these job-offer scenarios. This obviously wasn't a transactional, one-and-done negotiation. It was going to have long-term repercussions and affect some serious intangibles, and if she wasn't careful she might have ended up with a deal that looked good by the numbers but caused a lot of misery and emotional distress.

When entering into a negotiation that is about more than price, you have to nail down what it is you're after. On the dark side of the spectrum we included interests as the first task in your preparation, but they're generally so simple (just money) that we don't spend more than a few moments on them. Over on the lighter side it's more complex, so there are multiple interests to consider. Same process as before, but more effort. You'll list a number of interests, but you need to be clear on the *why* of the situation.

If we were to dissect this doctor's motivation in her negotiation, we would have to account for the fact that her interest was to find a position that allows for a lifestyle that's going to make relocation sustainable. Money was definitely part of the equation, but in this field, and given her needs, the difference in salaries wasn't going to influence her one way or another. She had a minimum salary she wanted to satisfy, and both options were going to hit it. More money wasn't going to make her happier; a lifestyle she could enjoy would. She was tired of studying around the clock and working crazy hours. She was ready for all of the hard work to pay off. She wanted to enjoy her work in a limited number of hours and still have time to enjoy the activities and hobbies that she'd been missing out on for so many years—including arts, culture, entertainment and travel.

If we had to sum up Paulina's interests going into these negotiations, they would look like this:

1. Manageable work schedule
2. Time to spend with friends and family

3. Access and time for hobbies and travel
4. Money to pay for her lifestyle

You can see that money was at the bottom of her list of interests; in a publicly funded system, the pay is relatively transparent, and she knew she had chosen a field that would guarantee a satisfactory financial reward, so it wasn't going to be a massive priority in these negotiations. As she thought about the other issues, they turned out to be the ones that would sway her the most. When she went down the list, thinking about how the remotely located job would satisfy each of those interests, it became harder and harder to picture.

The work schedule would be okay, since it wasn't a crazy busy market and the hospital was able to give her so much vacation time that she could often take long weekends. The time to spend with friends and family would be difficult, since she would have to make new friends in both locations. But getting her friends and family to come visit northern Canada was going to be difficult, both because it wasn't an appealing tourist destination and because flights were expensive and inconvenient. With the abundance of well-priced and well-timed flights to the vacation destination, it would be much easier for visitors to reach her.

Of course, the remote geography also posed a problem for her hobbies and travel. She'd have to tack on an extra day—wherever she was going—to accommodate the connecting flights and tricky timing required to get out of the north. And as this city wasn't close to any other metropolitan area, there was a limit to the arts and culture she might look forward to indulging in when she was finished work.

Prioritizing these elements was essential so that she was making decisions based on the factors that were most important to her, thus ensuring maximum satisfaction. Even if she managed to stay in Toronto, where she had access to her friends and all of the hobbies her heart desired, it would have been a horrible existence if she was working around the clock, unable to enjoy that access. When we pause to consider her Why—her motivation in this decision-making process—her quality of life was what consistently came up. Each of those issues served a greater Why: quality of life.

WEIGHTING YOUR ISSUES

Many folks struggle with the intangible component of these more complex negotiations, so for you spreadsheet junkies, here's a quick tool you can use to help you sort through your issues. List all of your issues, rank them, and then use a point system to give each one a weighting. I prefer to use a total of 100 to make the math easy. How many points would you give to a manageable work schedule, as opposed to access to hobbies or vacation time? If you know that a work schedule that doesn't leave you exhausted is the most important factor by far, then make sure it gets a lot of points. If money is trivial, then give it a trivial number of points. Distribute the leftovers among the rest of the issues as you see fit. Paulina's list could look like this:

1. Manageable work schedule—50 points
2. Time to spend with friends and family—25 points
3. Access and time for hobbies and travel—20 points
4. Money to pay for her lifestyle—5 points

As she starts considering some of the options that could help her solve for these interests, the point values will help her gauge how much time and energy to spend on each, which to emphasize, and which ones she'd be willing to sacrifice if push comes to shove.

DEFINING THEIR ISSUES

Of course, just as we did on the dark side of the negotiation, we need to pause to consider the interests of the other party. Without getting into the politics or details of how each medical system works, Paulina could have spent some time understanding the hospitals' interests to see if there was any compatibility between her list and theirs.

The remote hospital could have a list of issues that looked like this:

1. Long-term contract (they didn't want to constantly have to look for new talent)
2. Coverage (minimum hours to cover patient needs)
3. Competence (track record of performance to minimize liabilities)
4. Off-hours accessibility (in case of patient questions)
5. Money (need to keep it within budget)

The list for the US hospital, working under a different financing model, might look a little different:

1. Profitability (doctor's ability to participate in a high volume of revenue-generating activities)

2. Credentials (to add to their reputation and attract more patients)
3. ER coverage (occasional availability for off-peak coverage)
4. Competence (they have risk managers in place to minimize this)
5. Money (if you're creating revenue, you'll naturally get paid more)

For both of the clinics, profits and work hours required would take on different priorities—as one would expect in a publicly funded environment versus one in the private sector. The doctor considering a negotiation with each hospital would have to spend some time learning about how they operate, what the environment is like, the pressures they face and how that affects everyone in the workplace in order to determine whether there will be a compatible working relationship.

Understanding the Why and the subsequent interests that serve that Why is a critical part of the preparation process as you get into more complicated and complex negotiations. Being able to pause to quickly identify your priorities when you're in the process of negotiating will ensure that you're not going off track and getting distracted by issues that may not be important. It's the best way to maximize value and satisfaction as you consider these complex scenarios. Being aware of *their* Why will help you identify the interests they're trying to satisfy and will help you determine whether there are areas of mutual interest or potential conflict. You'll already have a sense of which areas will be collaborative, and therefore don't need to be negotiated, and which ones might be areas of conflict that you need to prepare to prevent or resolve as necessary. Preparing the issues for both sides is, once again, the first step in your negotiation on the light side—as it was on the dark side—but being more complex, this type will inevitably take a little more thought to complete.

CHAPTER 22

WHAT INFORMATION AM I WORKING WITH?

IDENTIFYING YOUR WHY AND YOUR ISSUES IS EASY enough. As always, what's going on inside the other person's head is still a bit of a mystery. You can make some educated guesses, as you did on the dark side of the spectrum, but as you progress across the spectrum and trust is developed, you may actually find the other party sharing information that takes some, if not all, of the guesswork out of it. If you've succeeded on this score, you'll be able to work more efficiently on the issues.

Before the negotiation even begins, you should have entered into some conversations about what's going on for both sides and why you're talking in the first place. Continuing with Paulina's story, the administrators at the clinics would have had some conversation with her about what interested her about their opportunities and what she envisioned for her career before they offered to fly her out for a discussion to sort through details. And she would have had plenty of questions for them in return before she invested the time and energy necessary to explore that option. But guess what: if you're cagey and closed and keeping your cards close to your vest, no one's going to want to open up to you. It's going to be difficult to treat this like a problem-solving opportunity if no one is being forthcoming about the problem. Misleading, lying or just plain being closed-off isn't going to get you far along the spectrum. Consider how you can spend a little time building trust and warming up the climate between you.

In section 1 we talked about some of the elements that help you move along the spectrum, and information was a major component. If the other side doesn't have any information about you, how do they know they can trust you? And the same is true for you: would you trust someone who is totally closed-off and not sharing anything? As you move along the spectrum, you also have to decide what information to share and what to hold back. As I mentioned earlier, you need information to figure out what to put into the value pie in order to grow it. But to ensure that they don't take advantage of you, you must also be mindful of not giving away too much (it's not as though you have *complete* trust in them—unless you're married, in which case, I hope you do).

Once again, in most cases it's likely appropriate to share the ranking of your priorities, but not necessarily the weighting you've assigned to those priorities. Paulina could go into the discussion saying, "Look, money is important to me, but it's even more important to me to find a manageable work schedule that's not going to leave me burned out in no time." Note that she's not saying, "Don't worry, money is not at all important to me, so go ahead and save your pennies and don't waste them on me." That would be crazy.

In order to avoid giving away too much information in the negotiation, you could add another element to your preparation process.

Divide a page into two sections: Information to share and Information to keep to yourself. Stuff you feel comfortable sharing (for example, your list of priorities) can be used to persuade them to reciprocate and share back. Stuff to keep to yourself is top secret because it would be harmful for them to know (for instance, how little you would be willing to accept in pay).

When I worked in the cosmetics industry, one of my buyers and I would negotiate every six months over support for a new product we were launching into the market. Every time a new mascara was going to be introduced, I'd have to go in there and talk to her about the volume, the type of displays we would be able to ship, the advertising support, and so many other items that were important to me, to her or to both of us. These conversations never involved the list price of the new product. Of course, she would ask all sorts of questions about the product, her thoughts turning on how she could maximize value (appropriately). Some of the things that were important to me included: persuading her to buy as many units as she possibly could, getting the best spot in the store to showcase our new product (to the detriment of my competitors) and getting it shipped at a time that would coincide with all of our TV advertising to make sure consumers could find it in stores when they saw the commercials. When I sorted through the information-sharing opportunity, I needed to be clear on what would be beneficial for me to share and what would be detrimental. I would share such details as:

- the general launch timing (this would make sure she was also set up to maximize her sales and would give her warning to prepare her stockrooms);

- forecasts and data on how well we expected the product to sell (which would make her want to buy more and get her to create room in her buying plan); and
- features of this new product that were yet to be shared with the public (which would get her excited and make her to want to support it in a big way).

What I *wouldn't* share were any of the details of our supply chain dates, our raw material costs and profit margins, or (duh) the patented formula that made the product unique.

Being clear on what information to share and what information is off-limits makes life a lot easier when you're in the middle of the conversation. You can easily press pause and figure out what's got a green light to share and a red light to keep in the vault. You may even have a yellow-light category that can't be determined until you build a little more trust.

Having some clear elements to share with the other party will start some crucial momentum down the trust road that will compel them to reciprocate with information of their own. Sometimes you may even want to share information they already know; just the act of sharing information, even if it's nothing new, creates a perception of trustworthiness that can be compelling enough to make them to open up. Though, as always, be sure that you understand your legal boundaries.

You also want to be prepared to respond when they ask you for information that you can't share. Snapping "I can't tell you that" is a surefire way to shut down communication. But saying, "While I'm not at liberty to discuss that, here's what I can share . . . " can create so much satisfaction that you make even more progress. If you can prepare a list of what information you won't be sharing, you can also prepare ways to work around those potential roadblocks.

CHAPTER 23

BRAINSTORMING YOUR WAY TO SOLUTIONS

YOU'VE GOT YOUR INTERESTS DOWN, YOU THINK YOU understand theirs, you're ready to start sharing and exchanging information, but there's still more information you may want to prepare before you go in. If you know the interests you're trying to meet, then consider what solutions could look like. Do some brainstorming. What measures could you—and they—take to solve your issues? Consider everything that could add value—for you and for them. Some will be quantitative (cash is often a factor, after all), but many will be qualitative because it is a value pie we're trying to grow. Give it a shot on your own and then bring the brainstorming to the negotiation table with you.

What does that look like? Take a blank sheet of paper (and I mean paper—get off the screen) and start writing ideas freely all over it. If your interest is to have a manageable schedule, consider pragmatically what that would look like. What can the other party do for you that would help? Could you work longer days from Monday to Thursday and take the occasional Friday off? Could they hire an administrative assistant to take on some of the filing that eats into your personal time? What about an extra week of vacation? Or a non-surgery day where you talk to patients from home via video chat instead of having to be in the clinic? Not long ago, that last one would have been considered unconscionable by many in the medical industry, so don't rule out even the kookiest ideas; brainstorming is meant to be creative, not discriminating though you'll (pause briefly to make sure you're not presenting anything that would hurt your credibility). Usually, there are no bad ideas, just a demonstration that you are ready to find creative solutions.

Of course, if you're truly going to treat this as a "we" negotiation, you'll want to consider options that will serve their needs as well. If credentials are important to them, you could agree to write a research paper once a year to help them fulfill that objective.

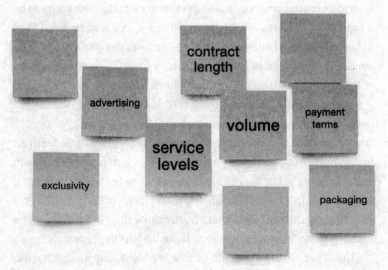

Figure 7: Brainstorming the variables that can be traded for value. More variables create more total value to be shared.

Or perhaps you could have a resident assigned to you to help you with that, thus minimizing the effort you'd have to put into it.

This brainstorming is going to make your move plan a lot easier. And the more ideas you have, the greater the value you can create and the more efficient and collaborative the negotiation will be.

ORGANIZING YOUR BRAIN

I always find brainstorming to be like making popcorn. Once you get started, the ideas start popping fast and furiously, and then they start . . . to . . . slow . . . down. If you feel like you've popped out all of your ideas and you're about to get burned out, take a pause and start organizing your thoughts. Weed out the ones that are a little too ridiculous, if you must; the ones that are left are each going to be a topic of conversation for your negotiation. You'll share this list of ideas with your counterpart, and you can both use it to start finding solutions. This agenda will not only help to make the conversation efficient (instead of spinning your wheels or talking in circles), but it is a wonderful tool to help you stay in charge of the negotiation process. It gives you some control and power because you're the one providing the topics of conversation. You want to give them an opportunity to contribute as well, of course, but don't count on them being as prepared or as creative as you are. You're the one taking the time to read this book, after all. So, you're likely putting more effort into this negotiation, and that effort results in getting more value than if neither of you had gone to these lengths to prepare.

The other great by-product of this agenda is that it creates trust. Think about it. If you've come to them with this list of issues that are not only important to you but also important to them—issues that can help them solve this problem you're facing together—then this would be perceived as an act of cooperation and trust. You've just inched your way a little farther along the spectrum toward greater value.

In formal situations, providing an agenda in advance, with an opportunity for them to add to it as well, is a great way to get the ball rolling and maintain control over the process. In less formal circumstances, an agenda is still going to be super-helpful even if it's not a written document. If you're sitting down with a family member at the kitchen table, pause to kick off the conversation in a collaborative way by saying, "There are a few things that I think would be beneficial to the both of us to discuss"—once again, demonstrating that this isn't a list serving just you, but the two of you. This will signal that you're considering their needs.

Acknowledgement and demonstrating that you've listened to them are important forms of satisfaction on this side of the spectrum. This dance looks a little different than on the other side. It's less about choreography and more about showing that you're paying attention to them. This agenda is also what helps you get across the dance floor. If you get stuck on one issue, you can park it, knowing you have a whole list of different areas you can work on. You won't get stuck anywhere for long if you have other steps that can get you moving again.

The agenda doesn't have to be tackled in any particular order; it's just a commitment to a list of topics you will cover at some point during the discussion. You can start with some easy ones to create momentum, or you can try to tackle the big ones right away, when you've got the most energy. Use it as your road map to move as you see fit.

Before you go in and just start winging the conversation about each topic on the agenda, you need to get a little more familiar with how this could play out. The thing about value-focused negotiations is that issues are usually more valuable to one party than to the other. And some of those requests can also be quite costly— even if the cost is intangible. An easy way to organize your thoughts before you have this conversation is to go through the issues you've brainstormed and sort them into categories; this will help you to quickly decipher which issues are important to them and which are important to you. It's another way to access your pause button when you're in the midst of the negotiation and the big jumbly mess of a brainstorm gets overwhelming.

I use a stoplight system to help sort through what is important to whom and what to do with that information.

> **Green:** They want stuff you can give. These issues are not important to you but are important to them, so it seems logical to give yourself the green light to give them that value. But just because you have it to give doesn't mean you should give it *easily*. Remember, even over here on the collaborative side of the spectrum, the other party is expecting a dance, so this is your chance to leverage the value you have to offer and create an *exchange* of value instead of just giving it away. Sit tight, because you're going to see why you'll need to use that value strategically instead of giving it away willy-nilly. You will give it away eventually, just not without thinking it through first.

Yellow: You want stuff they can give. These issues are not important to them but are important to you. But slow down and manage your expectations. Because they're anticipating the dance, they might be playing hard to get (yup, even in the collaborative negotiations). Just because they *can* give it to you, it doesn't mean they will just hand it over easily. They're going to be waiting for something in exchange. Good thing you didn't just give away those green-light issues, because you need to be prepared to trade something for these ones, which *are* important to you.

Figure 8: Every brainstormed variable gets categorized into the "traffic light" system to be sorted into proposals.

Red: You both want the same stuff. Brace yourself. These issues are important to you *and* to them. They're the ones that could get you feeling quite combative at times. If money is a component of this negotiation, it will fall into this category. You'll need to anticipate these issues before they derail you and force you back over to the dark side. Instead of getting caught up in an argument, consider how you can use some of those green-light issues here to entice the other party to budge from their red-light issues.

Trading is an important component of moving to the lighter side of the negotiation spectrum. And being able to identify where the most effective trades are is critical to your success. You don't want to accidentally trade away something that was important to you because you were overwhelmed in the moment. Plan to create pause buttons along the way.

CHAPTER 24

HOW DO I MOVE COLLABORATIVELY?

MAKING MOVES ON THE DARK SIDE WAS EASY ONCE WE became familiar with the basic concept of making moves of decreasing size—something that is done as part of the dance, one of the many rituals we perform to manage expectations. But now that we've entered "we" territory, we're no longer playing that tug of war; we're focusing on exchanges. And with so many intangibles in play, these "lighter" negotiations may not feel very light. That's because they're messy. Complex. Complicated. But you've already learned to simplify them by identifying your Whys and your interests, brainstorming solutions, and sorting through what to give and which obstacles to be aware of.

Your next step is to get your moves ready. If you're going to succeed at making trades, it's time to implement the four magic words of negotiation. If you can make these words a regular part of your vocabulary, I guarantee you'll see a dramatic improvement in your negotiations—and the way you resolve everyday conflicts. So, are you ready for it? I mean *really* ready? If there's one thing you use most from this book, I hope this is it (besides the pause, because I think I've imprinted on your brain how ridiculously important it is). Here are the four life-changing magic words that create value:

IF YOU . . .   THEN I . . .

IF YOU can do *this* [insert yellow- or red-light issue] for me, THEN I can do *this* [insert green-light issue] for you.

Voilà! You've just learned the art of *conditional trading*. The condition is that you get something for giving something. This trading of concessions prevents anyone from taking advantage of you (they won't assume that you're just giving stuff away, so they won't get greedy for more). It also creates the satisfaction they're looking for. They expected a dance, and though the steps may be a little different over on this side of the spectrum, these four words are the choreography that allow you to create satisfaction and move across the dance floor.

The order here is super-important. IF YOU do this thing that I want, THEN I can do this thing that you want. Take care of *your* needs first—flip the *E* around for your benefit first, then flip it around for them. If you don't, they'll only hear, "I'll do this thing for you," and they'll likely stop listening because they just heard that they got what they wanted. They are already dancing for joy and/or plotting what else they can get out of you since, damn, that was easy. You'll either not get the chance to finish the exchange because they've already moved on to something else, or you're about to hit them with the other half of that sentence: ". . . but only if you do this thing for me." If you do that, you're slapping them across the face with a punishment. *But* is a dangerous word. It gets backs up against the wall.

It makes us brace for a problem. It feels ominous. And in this case, with good reason. You've just punished them! You might as well be wagging your finger at them like a schoolteacher scolding a child.

Let's consider a basic example. You're at the coffee shop with a friend and the tables are almost full. One of you had better grab a table before someone else in line gets the last one, so your friend says, "I'll wait for the coffees, but only if you go get a table." How rude! When did she lose her manners? What are you to her that she thinks she can speak to you that way—a child? Ugh. The nerve of some people!

But what if she had said, "If you get a table, I'll wait here for the coffees"? You'd think, "Oh, that makes sense. I'd be happy to go get a table for us." Unlike the first example, this is an appropriate exchange of energy and value. You're both happy with the outcome, and I bet you didn't even realize you were in a negotiation. Same trade, different reaction. The perception of a punishment versus a gift is an important factor in delivering satisfaction. Taking care of your needs first will actually make the other party more satisfied, because you'll be finishing the exchange with what sounds like a gift, leaving a sweet taste in their mouth instead of a sour one.

Those of you with kids will find this particularly valuable.

"IF YOU clean the garage, THEN I will let you borrow the car.

"IF YOU eat all of your vegetables, THEN I will give you dessert."

"IF YOU stop screaming, THEN I won't give away all of your toys." Too far? Maybe. But you get my point.

Just be warned: as I've said before, turning everything into a creative negotiation could condition your kids to assume that everything is negotiable. Sometimes Mom and Dad just need to lay down the law, and that's okay. Other times, why not encourage creative solutions and get your kids to think outside the box instead of assuming they'll get whatever they want? You decide the balance.

Those four magic words will help you out of some real jams if you get the order right. Taking care of your needs first and finishing with a gift for the other side is the key. To tackle more complicated negotiations, or the ones that have more than just one simple "if you" and one "then I," you just need to prepare a list of moves. Divide a page in half and write IF YOU at the top of the left-hand column and THEN I at the top of the right. So far, so good? Great.

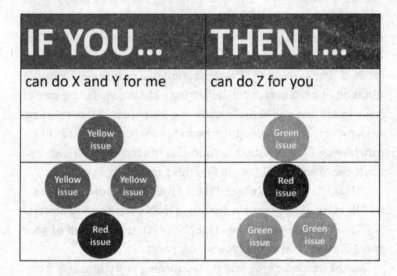

Figure 9: Map out your red-, yellow- and green-light issues, always making sure that the value of your "if you" portion of the proposal is greater than the cost of your "then I" portion.

Remember, the "if you" items are things that will take care of your needs—the things that you want. These are the things you've put in the yellow and red categories. This is your opportunity to frame them up in an exchange that will entice the other party to dance with you. So, list all of your red- and yellow-light specials in the left-hand column, and then take all of those green lights that you can give away and put them into the right-hand column. It doesn't matter which ones you match up as long as you're *never giving away more than you're getting in return*.

For example, you wouldn't tell your kid, "If you put your dishes in the dishwasher [something he or she should have been doing anyway], then I will get you a new bike." What? Rewarding them for a task so minor, they should have been doing it anyway? Make sure you're getting something of equal or greater value with this formula, or you're conditioning them to do nothing and expect rewards for it. The same is true when you're at the office. "If you can hold the door open for me, then, yes, I will do that five-hour project you've been asking about." Huh? Save some of that for later. Your time and energy are valuable; what can you do to make sure they aren't taken for granted?

Imagine if you gave your dog a treat every time they did something that merited a reward. You'd condition the pup to continue performing this way. But if you gave the dog the whole box of treats for doing nothing, you'd probably leave your pet wanting more. And when that box is empty and they are still expecting more, brace yourself for some bad behavior. Do dogs have temper tantrums too, or is that just toddlers? I don't have dogs (or kids), but I've seen what poor expectation management can do to adults, and it ain't pretty. The bottom line is: make sure you're managing expectations before everyone expects you to drop everything to work on their five-hour projects.

Of course there are exceptions to this policy. Nothing is black and white. Sometimes you need to create goodwill; sometimes you just want to do something nice for people. That's great. Go you! My goal is to plant a little seed of awareness so that you have something to think about before you find yourself in a position where you ask yourself, "Why am I working late every night while my coworker is the one getting promoted?" Maybe every once in a while, you can throw out an offer like "If you can help me figure out how to get one of these other projects off my plate, then I'd be happy to help with your challenge." Expectation managed.

REACTING TO MOVES ON THE LIGHTER SIDE

You're ready for the basic collaborative negotiations that you encounter all the time, but with your list of "if you . . . then I" moves, you're also ready for the complicated ones. When you go into your negotiation, bring your list of moves with you, and use it the same way you would the moves on the "me" side of negotiation.

Make a Proposal → Allow Them to Digest It →
Let Them Counter-propose → Acknowledge Their Proposal → Repeat

Let's talk about that acknowledgment for a moment. On the darker side of the spectrum, you needed to make sure they saw a reaction lest they stay on course to try to separate you from all of your cash. That acknowledgment provided satisfaction to them because it indicated they were getting everything they could out of you and that they needed to work harder to get a good deal. You likely shook your head and used the word *no* a lot. Over here, however, we have a warmer climate. We have relationships to think about and we want to keep everyone motivated to work toward a solution. That doesn't mean you become a yes man/woman. You still need to get them to keep improving their proposals until you get to something that satisfies both of you. But they need encouragement instead of discouragement. You can still show exasperation if you're getting frustrated, but you always want to maintain an environment where you're working toward progress. If you're frustrated that they're not moving with you, there's no harm in letting out a sigh or a look that shows you're perplexed, but you don't want to be insulting. You can acknowledge their proposal by saying, "I appreciate your trying to work with me; here's what I can do to make this work: If you . . . then I . . ."

It's as if you're putting a bunch of puzzle pieces on the table and slowly moving them around together until you create a picture that works for both parties. You might find yourself adding moves to your list, or building on theirs as these "pieces" fit into your picture of value. If you keep making these moves, eventually you'll get to a place where both of you feel satisfied to agree.

A MOVING SHORTCUT: MESOS

When you're dealing with a whole bunch of issues and it seems like it's going to take forever to move all of the puzzle pieces into place, there is a tool that can help you create value, gather more information and manage a collaborative environment while fast-tracking the proposal process. Damn, that's a lot to get done. Before you get too excited about it, bear in mind that it takes a lot of preparation and should be done at the *beginning* of the negotiation process. This tool is the concept of *multiple equivalent simultaneous offers*—known as MESOs. Sounds like a mouthful, but it's actually easy. It's taking a bunch of those "if you . . . then I" statements and presenting them at the same time in the form of options.

Let's start with a simple example. Instead of fighting with your kids about eating their vegetables, you can approach them with a MESO. "Would you like to have broccoli or cauliflower with your dinner?" By giving them multiple offers simultaneously, you make them feel like they have some autonomy, which gives them immense levels of satisfaction. It also gives you a chance to find out a little more about their preferences and habits.

If you want to make things a little more complex, you can ask, "Would you like broccoli, spinach and carrots on your plate, or cauliflower, peas and carrots?" Whichever answer they give you, it's an opportunity to ask follow-up questions like "What do you like better about the second plate?" Maybe you'll find out that they think foods that are green are going to turn them into a frog, so they chose the plate with fewer green things. Or maybe they just hate mushy things, so they chose the one with the crispy spinach. They could (and will likely) tell you they hate both options. Once again, it's your chance to ask some questions and say, "But which one of these is the better one of the two, and why? Let's see if we can make some adjustments to make it even better." It's your tool to learn a little more about what's important to them or what they would prioritize (taste . . . texture . . . color?).

The same will happen with adults in all sorts of situations. There is a benefit to starting the conversation with these MESOs to find out more information and make adjustments to the picture until all the pieces fit well. I recently spoke to an accountants' association. Many of the members of this group had clients they've been working with for years, if not decades. These weren't exactly darker negotiations, and yet they were concerned about how to raise their prices. They knew that news of the change wouldn't be easy to deliver. We talked about ways to frame the negotiation to make clients feel like they had some autonomy and help to understand what was most important to them. They could lay out three options:

Package 1: Stay with the current rate.
   a) Remove the on-call, ad hoc advisory service for questions, limiting the service to one assessment/year.
   b) Remove the bookkeeping service that was previously included.
   c) Additional appointments and bookkeeping are available for a fee.

Package 2: Choose price increase of 8 percent, with no other changes
   a) Keep the on-call service.
   b) Keep the bookkeeping service.

Package 3: Choose price increase of 13 percent, and get full service

a) Keep the on-call service.
b) Keep the bookkeeping service.
c) Add monthly automated reports.
d) Add audit insurance (no additional fees if you get audited and require help).

Providing—and getting feedback on—these options allows the accountant to understand each client's priorities. Package 1 is obviously all about the lowest possible cost and offers the most basic service. Package 2 prioritizes some conveniences. Package 3 adds a layer of risk management. If a client asks questions about the third package, you know they are less concerned about price and are likely risk-averse. This conversation could lead to another creative option that you hadn't thought of. It's also a chance for them to learn a little more about how much time and energy goes into the accounting services you provide, as well as what else you could offer. This information exchange is valuable to both of you at the beginning of the discussion as you work through questions and answers, perhaps even introducing more creative ideas, to get to a solution that will satisfy both parties for the long term. Maybe you can give them a trial of the monthly automated reports, allowing them to see the value of the service and perhaps get hooked.

If you start doing the negotiation dance and then drop these packages at the end of your allotted time, it will feel like a dump of information when your counterpart is already stressed and overwhelmed—and could be perceived as a deceitful tactic. You will also have missed an opportunity to learn more about what would get you and your client to a better and more efficient deal.

As I mentioned before, preparation is critical to using this method successfully, because you'll have to carefully lay out multiple options for them to choose from. You'll have to balance out each option to make it clear you're happy to accept whichever one is chosen. When you present them, you'll have to take things nice and slow so that the other party has time to digest *all* of this complex information you're about to dump on them. "I've been thinking about ways to help us moving forward. I've come up with a few options to walk you through, and once we've gone through them, I'd like to get your feedback on which would be the best option."

Odds are, like the kids, they won't like any option as it is; instead, they'll likely want to make adjustments, but guess what? You've anchored an awesome starting point that will have them dancing around *your* options—the ones *you* put on the table. With the kids, you're getting them to eat vegetables; they didn't have a chance to mention candy as an option because we started down the veggie path. With the adults, they're going to be molding and working around the options that you put on the table instead of dragging you somewhere completely different from where you want to be.

MESOs are a great way to:

- build trust
- anchor
- gather information
- create efficiencies

Put in the preparation time up front and take the time to pause frequently as everyone digests all of the adjustments, and you'll complete a picture of satisfaction. You'll find you're moving across the dance floor in no time. My students constantly credit MESOs with their success in the classroom, the boardroom and at home. It takes some practice to use them effectively, but the effort is well worth it. In my consulting practice, we use MESOs frequently to force some more collaborative behavior from the other party. Remember, most of the clients who call me are doing so because they know they're going to be dealing with difficult negotiators or they're already stuck in a rut. MESOs are frequently the way to prevent combative and competitive behavior and are often the key to unlocking valuable information to help us move forward. Even in the most elementary form (broccoli or cauliflower?), people love having choices. It gives them the perception of control, even though you're the one choosing vegetables over candy for them!

GOING BACK TO WHY

Of course, even in this complicated type of negotiation, you still want to remember to frame the proposal(s) from their perspective. Go back to the E exercise we did earlier. What does success look like for the client? What would motivate them to want to move in your direction? What's driving their behavior? Your E is that you need to make a better profit. You're spending too much time on their work and not making enough money. That won't exactly motivate them to want to pay more. But their E could be that they want to maintain the same level of service. Alternatively, their E might be to keep their costs low. Or it might be all about reducing their risk of surprise additional costs. Consider who you're dealing with and the perspective they're coming from. Consider their Why and start there. The accountants would be able to set the stage this way, with a little inspiration from Simon Sinek's Golden Circle:[8]

Why (the *E* that is driving their behavior): "Hey client, we're working on ways to make sure we can continue to provide all of our clients with our consistently high level of service. To do that, we're making some changes, and we've carved out some ways to make sure you still feel like you're getting the best value and pricing for your needs."

How (the process): "We wanted to make sure we gave you plenty of time to consider your needs and ask us any questions to ensure that we're meeting those needs so, on January 1 we're rolling out some new service plans to choose from."

What (the proposal): "Package 1 is . . ."

Closing (the key to keeping the conversation collaborative): "When is the best time to discuss your preferred options?"

Framing options in terms of the other party's Why is more likely to get them to consider—and agree to—your proposals. It's also a great way to coax them into moving along the collaborative side of the spectrum with you. Structuring your communication is such an important component of getting what you want, and that's where we're headed in the next chapter. Once you've got the perspective and structure down, it's time to work on finessing what specifically to say during the process.

PAUSE FOR REFLECTION

SECTION 5 | THE PROCESS OUR WAY: THE COLLABORATIVE SIDE
CHECKLIST OF KEY TAKEAWAYS

✓ **Value is the priority.** Money is not the top priority on the "we" side; value is.

✓ **Dig a little deeper.** Go beneath the surface to get to the interests, then open up options to serve them.

✓ **Satisfaction in Our Way negotiations manifests itself differently.** Over here, satisfaction sometimes just means listening—acknowledgment creates satisfaction and is *not* the same thing as agreement.

✓ **Sort out your information.** Determine what information to share and what to keep secret as you move along the spectrum, and prepare how to respond when they ask you for information you don't want to share.

✓ **Brainstorm value sources.** Get ready to sort through the more complex side of the spectrum by brainstorming what measures could solve both your issues and theirs—valuable stuff for you *and* for them. Some variables will be quantitative, but there are definitely going to be qualitative ones on this side.

- ✓ **Categorize your variables.** Identify which variables are for giving away (your green-light items), which you are trying to get from them (yellow-light items) and which are too costly to give up (red-light items).
- ✓ **Weight your issues.** Trade effectively to make sure you're not giving away more value (in the form of green-light items) than you're getting in return (in red- or yellow-light ones).
- ✓ **Make it conditional.** Frame proposals in the form of "if you . . . then I . . ." language to deliver satisfaction and keep discussions collaborative. The other side needs to feel like they're getting something out of it, and framing proposals as a gift instead of a punishment is the way to do it. Options are a great way to deliver satisfaction here—they feel like they have autonomy instead of doing things your way.
- ✓ **Pause.** It is important here for building satisfaction and trust.

SECTION 6

COMMUNICATE LIKE A PRO

CHAPTER 25

EFFECTIVE COMMUNICATION COMPONENTS

YOU'VE MADE IT. YOU KNOW WHAT YOU WANT. YOU'VE thought about what they want. Interests aligned (if possible)? Check. BATNAs? Check. You've got a process. Moves ready? Check. So, what else is there? In this section, we'll discuss ways to use verbal and nonverbal language effectively so that you send the intended messages. We'll also touch on some bad verbal habits to avoid, ways to bring a discussion back on track, and questions that work well.

IT STARTS WITH THE MINDSET

You think you're ready to go and then . . . it happens. Brain freeze. What . . . the heck . . . do I actually say? How do I make sure I'm not spewing out verbal diarrhea? How do I make them believe the words that are coming out of my mouth?

My clients often joke that they'd love to just wear an earpiece and have me feeding them lines, but the fact is, even if I tell you what to say, if you're not mentally prepared and authentic, my script would be a flop. You need that self-assured mindset to execute the go-to phrases and tips we'll be exploring in this chapter with credibility.

Your pause button is the key to your success before, while and after you send messages. Once you put yourself out there and start communicating with the other person, you are sending all sorts of messages and information their way. Some of it, you're sending intentionally. Some of it, not so much. Without the pause button, your nerves will start taking over your brain, your tongue and your other body parts and start sending all sorts of mixed messages. The good news is that planning and practice truly do help get that mindset under control.

Preparation activates the pause button. Consider what it's like to go into a negotiation and get ready to make a proposal to your new employer that will affect your salary by thousands of dollars a year (no pressure). You don't want to be spitting out those words for the first time when you're a bundle of nerves. But practicing, whether in front of a mirror or with a friend, will give your brain a little bit of muscle memory so that your mouth doesn't get tongue-tied. And that muscle memory is a pause button. The knowledge that you sounded like a sane and credible person when you practiced? That's another pause button. Taking the time to consider how they might respond and what you will do in that situation? Still another one.

Just knowing that you've done the work and that you know what to expect goes a long way. After all, knowledge is power, and the knowledge that you're not guessing your way through this negotiation is powerful stuff. With the preparation under your belt, you'll be able to communicate with ease when the time comes for the real deal.

HOW WE SEND MESSAGES

When it comes to those messages that the conscious and subconscious minds are sending, we communicate in three ways: we use our words, our sounds and our body language. A pair of famous studies on communication by the noted psychologist Albert Mehrabian investigated the ways these three elements affect the way we perceive the speaker. He found that the actual words that are spoken account for only 7 percent of the message, while tone of voice accounts for 38 percent and body language for 55 percent. These findings have stirred up their fair share of controversy over the years. Some have interpreted Mehrabian's results as meaning that words are relatively unimportant. Others—including Dr. Mehrabian himself—have cautioned against using these results to make any blanket assumptions about the power of each form of communication. I bring the study up in case you find yourself at a cocktail party and want to start spewing this shaky statistical myth. My advice: just don't.

What you *can* share with your friends and colleagues—and maybe that crush you want to impress—is that we use all three methods of communication to express ourselves. Telling someone that words are insignificant would be a mistake. Try saying that to someone who's been up all night trying to figure out why their baby won't stop crying. "WHAT DO YOU WANT FROM ME?" the parent pleads. "I've fed you, changed you, and you won't stop crying!" Some words from that distressed baby would be helpful for that person right about now.

But as helpful as words can be, we can't always trust that they're accurate. It doesn't take a scientist to figure out that whenever you get a sense that a loved one isn't in a great mood and you ask them if they're okay, if they respond, "I'm fine" through clenched teeth and folded arms, they're really not. And soon enough, you'll find out that neither are you. The one insight from Mehrabian's studies that communication experts can agree on is the insight that if the three modes of communication are sending conflicting messages, we're most likely to believe the person's body language. Those clenched teeth are far more compelling than the words "I'm fine."

And if one or two of these modes of communication are missing, the example of the screaming baby shows us how there could be room for misinterpretation. If the baby starts bobbing their head against your chest, it could mean that they're looking for their next meal. It could also mean you're not supporting their head well. If the baby starts making the same wailing noise that they do for their 3 a.m. feeding, it's more likely that you've interpreted correctly that it's feeding time. But there's still a chance that the wailing is a signal of discomfort, and if it could, the baby would be yelling, "Support my head, you idiot!" Who knows? What we do know is that it would be a lot easier to understand that child if they were able to use words to communicate.

It's a lot easier to understand each other as adults if we use all three methods of communication—intentionally and competently. It is so much easier to build and measure trust when you're face to face with someone and have the luxury of not only hearing the sincerity in their tone, but also seeing the look on their face. It's difficult to build trust through email or text messages. Even in the online dating world, at some point you need to meet the person to see if they're the real deal. But there are pros and cons to each method of communication. To be an effective negotiator, you need to be aware of all of these circumstances so that you can maximize your chances of success.

If you've got the luxury of all three methods of communication, then you're less likely to make a mistake in interpreting their messaging and you're more likely to send a consistent message to the other party; I always advocate face-to-face communication to collect the most data you can—think about what you might miss out on if you're constantly hiding behind a text-only screen. But when that's not possible—if you're a nervous Nellie, for example—then pause to consider your next best option and choose the communication method that will work best for you under the circumstances.

CHAPTER 26

THE WRITTEN WORD

HEY, I GET IT. IN A GLOBAL SOCIETY WITH TELECOMMUTING and technology at our fingertips, it's not always optimal or even possible to have every interaction face to face. We've become so dependent on our smartphones, laptops and other devices that it's easier to just drop someone a line than pick up a phone or (gasp!) walk all the way over to their desk. We use technology in the name of efficiency, even when it's not efficient. And if someone misinterprets your instructions or mistakenly thinks you were insulting them, you send another message to apologize for the misunderstanding—then wait anxiously for their reply and figure out how to repair the damage caused by that interaction. Which assumes they even got your original instant message in the instant you sent it. You may have to wait until they've noticed the indicator light flashing—or they've replied to the twelve other emails in the queue ahead of yours.

Depending on communicating by email or text message may not be a big deal if the stakes are low, trust isn't required and time isn't of the essence. For something super-simple, it may not be worth your time to travel to a face-to-face meeting. Or maybe you just want to drop a note at some odd hour—say, when an idea has popped into your head and you don't want to risk forgetting or waiting around to call the other person when they wake up or get out of their meetings. You just want to get something off your plate and make sure you've done your duty in letting them know. Cool. Perhaps you get fidgety and nervous when talking to people, even if just on the phone, so it's easier for you to communicate via the written word. I understand. That may be the best reason I've heard for depending on email and text. The major benefit of using email instead of speaking to a live human being is to mitigate the anxiety that can accompany that social interaction. It's like having unlimited use of the pause button. Why wouldn't you want to do everything by email?

The downside to depending on written messages is that, if the other party doesn't have access to your tone of voice and facial expressions, it's so damn easy for them to misinterpret your intentions. If you're sarcastic, try sending someone a message dripping in sarcasm and cross your fingers that they pick up on it. There's always a chance they'll think you're a weirdo. For example, if you were to ask me how writing this book is going, I might answer, "It's great. I love working on weeknights and weekends. I have no interest in having a social life." A new parent might say, "I just love waking up to feed the baby multiple times a night." There may be the odd enamored new mom who actually does feel this way. But there are plenty of others who don't. Perhaps an emphasis on *looove*, combined with a roll of the eyes, could signify that they're being sarcastic. But you don't get those clues in a text message.

Can you imagine getting an email from a colleague responding to your idea by saying, "Oh yeah, the client is just going to love that"? You go merrily on your way, preparing your presentation, not realizing that they were being sarcastic. You've now wasted your time and looked foolish. Sarcasm, like most other emotions, is hard to infer from a text message. Writing this book has been a real challenge for me because I am so animated when I'm on stage or at the front of a classroom (just look online for any photos of me in action—I look a little crazy in all of them!) and it's hard to bring that quality to the written word. Are you listening to it in my voice? Is my emphasis coming across? Am I as funny if you can't see my weird facial expressions? All a mystery. I have no clue how the tone is landing. Grammar and punctuation also become super-important: "Let's eat, Grandma" versus "Let's eat Grandma" is one of my favorite examples. Are you telling her to join you or is she the main course? That comma sure changes the game! You get the point.

Think of it this way: every mode of communication you're missing increases the probability that you could be misinterpreted. So, if you're going to depend solely on your words, you had better make the most of them and pause to make sure that you've thought carefully about what you're going to say, so as to minimize confusion. When the pressure is on, that's when you're more tempted to be quick with the send button, but it's always a good idea to simmer down. This is the time when you need to pause the most. Autocorrect will be your worst nightmare if you don't slow down. I've received some awkward messages that were not meant for me. I've also received messages that were addressed to Fontini, Fortini and

Fontina (I . . . am not . . . a cheese). Sending a greeting with an incorrect spelling may be an innocent mistake, but it is likely to be interpreted, even if only subconsciously, as meaning that you didn't even care enough to get my name right, so why should I listen to anything you say? Yikes.

You'll want to be careful about starting off the note on the right foot. Need to be on the lighter side of negotiation? Take a second to warm up the climate by writing a greeting, giving a compliment or generating some positive vibes before launching into your request; otherwise, you will be perceived as abrasive. When I worked in a consulting firm, before I had control over my own schedule, life was chaotic. I'd be with clients and would find myself running to squeeze in the next training module, to jump on a call—or even to catch a flight. Like the other consultants, I had little time to converse with my peers and colleagues in the office. Any time I did have was earmarked for clients. When I did need to reach out to the administrator in the office, I was sending off super-quick notes in the name of efficiency. They'd look something like this:

Hey Maria,

Customer X just called and they need a date change. Please make the adjustment and send out the appropriate materials.

Thanks,
Fotini

Emails like this were common from the road-warrior consultants, and phone calls sounded pretty similar. When you're literally running from point A to point B (and try doing that in stilettos), there's not a lot of time or energy for pleasantries. I wasn't getting the response rate I was anticipating, even though I knew this woman was sharp. When I was in the office (one of the rare occasions I wasn't on a clock), I had a chat with Maria about why she wasn't responding. Her response surprised me. She found my notes rude and she didn't feel that they deserved a response. Wow. I thought making sure I said please and thank you insulated me from being perceived as rude. But there's always room for interpretation otherwise. She also had no idea that I was so limited on time when I was dropping her these notes (not that it ever excuses rudeness), so it didn't leave any room for her to react by thinking, "Oh, Fotini must be super-busy if her note is so short. She's usually much more pleasant."

You can't necessarily control how the other party's brain works, but you *can* influence it and reduce the odds of being misinterpreted. It's worth taking the extra moments to do so. In this workplace example, it took way more of my time and energy to wonder whether the change had been made, and then calling and confirming it—never mind the increased stress that resulted from chasing the issue. I needed to pause to pay a little more attention to my messages and how they could be seen in a more positive light. Spending a few extra seconds (no exaggeration) on my note could have had a much different result:

Hey Maria,

Hope you're having a great day. Mine is a little chaotic and I can use your help making sure that customer X stays happy while I try to juggle the other client I'm working with today. Customer X needs a date change. Can you please follow up with them to make the adjustment and send out the appropriate materials?

Thanks for your help,
Fotini

If you think typing an extra forty-two words is too much in the name of efficiency, think again. Those forty-two words take an average of a minute; compare that with the cost of someone becoming irritated with you, which will not only include the time spent on a follow-up phone call (or multiple rabbit-hole emails), but the effort you'll need to invest in repairing the damage to the relationship when you're trying to undo her perception that you are a jerk who doesn't deserve her attention. I spent a few minutes chatting with Maria about her expectations and filling her in on my crazy limitations and schedule. The time I invested in that conversation—plus my new email style—not only repaired the relationship but also prevented future misunderstandings. Because of my pause to correct the situation, and my subsequent few moments of pausing whenever I sent a note, I became the consultant whose issues were prioritized ahead of the rest of the bunch. A little pause goes a long way. If someone doesn't have the benefit of the sound of your voice or the look on your face, you need to make sure every single one of those words counts.

You'll notice that with my forty-two extra words, I added a little warmth (showing some concern about her day) and included a common Why (the need to keep the customer happy) to make her more receptive to the request. This may seem trivial, but it was a negotiation for her time and effort, and one that would save me more of the same. Why would she want to collaborate with me if I wasn't exhibiting the behaviors associated with the relationship and trust of a "we" negotiation? I thought the word *please* was the indicator of collaboration, but it wasn't enough. It might have been for one of my consulting colleagues who communicated the same way and came from the same set of circumstances, but it wasn't for this other person. Leave less room for error by pausing to choose your words carefully.

SAY LESS, GET MORE

One of my favorite funny negotiation stories comes from a friend who watched an exchange on an airplane. To set the scene, a couple were traveling together, but they were separated—one in the window seat and one on the aisle, with a stranger sitting between them in the dreaded middle seat. No one actually likes the middle seat, do they? The aisle seat gives you room to stretch out into the aisle and quick access to the bathroom without climbing over anyone; plus, you're the first to get out when it's time to deplane. The window seat (my preference) gives you somewhere to lean when you want to sleep, and it's the ideal spot if you don't want to be disturbed by people climbing over you; plus, you get a decent view of the outside world and control over the window shade. What's the middle seat got? Nada. Unless your loved one is sitting next to you—assuming you like their company.

The couple asked the woman if she would trade her middle seat for the aisle seat. They assumed she'd be happy with the trade—surely she'd think that anything was better than sitting in the middle. They were surprised when she politely said, "I'll take the window seat if you two want to sit together." The couple repeated their offer of the aisle. To which she responded, clearly and diplomatically, "I'm offering to move into the window seat to let you sit together." For whatever reason, which she had no need to explain, she wasn't interested in the aisle seat. One could say that *anything* would be an improvement over the middle, but she was aiming to trade *all the way* up. And why not? Who had the power here? She had nothing to lose, since she was already prepared to sit in the middle seat. Meanwhile, the couple were motivated to switch seats because it seemed silly for them to stay separated when the opportunity for a change existed.

The funniest part of this, according to my friend, was the dumbfounded look on the faces of the couple. They kept trying to persuade the woman that *anything* would be better than the middle seat. And she just paused and calmly stuck by her counteroffer: "If you give me the window seat, then you can sit together." Her language was clear and concise. She wasn't rude; she was matter-of-fact, even collaborative (using "if you, then I" language). While most people in this situation would have assumed that they'd have no choice but to accept the couple's offer, she was patient enough to hit the pause button. She didn't say anything that would make her seem unreasonable; nor did she signal that she was willing to compromise. In this basic transactional negotiation, her brief counterproposal made her so much more powerful without draining her battery with unnecessary words. Her clear language paid off when the couple got to sit together and she got a great view from the window. A win-win scenario in which the view gave the single traveler a win that was a little bigger.

When you're making proposals in general, but particularly when you're making "dark side" proposals that have to do with price, you want to make sure that you protect that perception of power. Remember that on the dark side, power is particularly important, but even if you have all the power in the world, if the other party perceives that you're operating with a drained battery, you could end up in a position of weakness.

Your words are a critical component of the negotiation process, so you want to make sure you choose them just as carefully in "me" negotiations as you do when you are warming up the climate for the more collaborative scenarios you face. On the competitive, darker side of negotiation, you're competing to win, so you need to use confident, winning language. Often, that means less language in general.

WHEN "SAY LESS" MEANS SILENCE

A few years ago I went from condominium living to house living, and at the beginning of my first winter in the house, I realized I hated shoveling snow with a passion and needed to outsource that task. It was a tiny home in downtown Toronto, which meant it had a teeny-tiny driveway. After I asked around, I expected it to cost $400 to have the driveway shoveled by a professional for the four months of winter. The kid across the street used to shovel for the previous owner for $200 for the winter. With my research done, I put up a post in a local Facebook group with some basic details and I got a few responses. This was one of them:

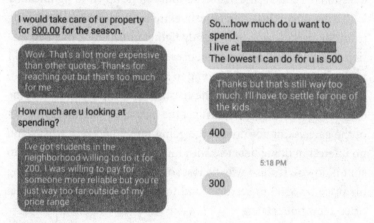

I would take care of ur property for 800.00 for the season.

Wow. That's a lot more expensive than other quotes. Thanks for reaching out but that's too much for me.

How much are u looking at spending?

I've got students in the neighborhood willing to do it for 200. I was willing to pay for someone more reliable but you're just way too far outside of my price range.

So....how much do u want to spend.
I live at ▮▮▮▮▮▮▮▮▮▮▮
The lowest I can do for u is 500

Thanks but that's still way too much. I'll have to settle for one of the kids.

400

5:18 PM

300

Figure 10: Pausing during the negotiation pays off.

I should mention that when I'm in full-day sessions with clients, I don't look at my phone, so this conversation started in the morning, and after I sent my last text (shutting down the negotiation), I put my phone away. Hours later, my inadvertent pause resulted in the snow removal guy negotiating against himself! While I was busy with clients, the snow guy was sweating out the loss of a potential client—that is what the power of pausing can do. You'll also notice that I didn't have to get rude or nasty to get results. Say less, get more.

There are a number of other issues in this exchange, including the fact that the gentleman asked me a question about how much I was willing to pay but didn't pause long enough to let me answer him and give him a proposal. Instead, he negotiated against himself and dropped his price by $300 without my having to answer the question. Of course, the reason he could come down so significantly is that he opened so ridiculously extreme. We were transitioning from the darkest side to a slightly lighter zone, since this negotiation was going to have consequences for the next four months and I needed to trust that he was going to show up every time it snowed. When you start to turn up the trust, you need to turn down the extremes, but this fellow didn't get the message. When he came out of the gate asking for double the going rate, I had zero trust—and no interest in doing business with him (that's why I politely tried to shut it down). It's also why he lost so much credibility by dropping his price by $300 in seconds, and to less than half of his original price a few hours later.

The lack of words helped me, and his verbose proposals hurt him. When he said, "The lowest I can do . . . ," it was a red flag to me. It's a common negotiation tactic that is often used to fake out negotiators. When I hear words like *lowest, highest, maximum, minimum, best* (or other language that suggests finality) paired with signals of mistrust (like extreme proposals), my automatic response is to think they can do better. And indeed he did. But when he crossed over the line he'd drawn in the sand, he killed his credibility, and every subsequent proposal lowered my satisfaction, making me wonder what his next "best" offer would be. The line moved once, so why wouldn't it move again? The lesson for you is to avoid super-fluous language, and unless it truly is your best offer, avoid phrases that suggest as much. When you hear words or phrases like that from someone else, ask yourself, "Is that *truly* their best offer, or is this a tactic?" People will give themselves away if you pause long enough to let them.

CHOOSE YOUR WORDS CAREFULLY

Before I sold my last house, I had to conduct a negotiation as I was looking for a quote for some minor renovations to my basement. The job was going to take a couple of days and I didn't have the time (or interest) to do it myself. The countertop in the tiny kitchen needed to be replaced, and there would a bit of mudding and paint-ing. Of course, I had already done some preparation for this negoti-ation by using a home improvement website to research how much the supplies would cost, and I had checked out a local app to find out about hourly rates for handy work in the area. Armed with the information, I knew I shouldn't spend any more than $600—this became my resistance point. (Remember, the resistance point is the point just before you walk away from this deal and head for your BATNA.) When a handyman came in to take a look at the job and give me a quote, he managed to anchor first.

"For this project," he said, "I think it might be somewhere around $700 to $800."

How firm or confident does this proposal sound to *you*? As I heard this, I recognized a few signals that this person was flexible and able to go even lower than his stated price range.

The words *I think* were a big flag. If I *think*, it means I don't know for certain. I'm unsure, so you can feel free to move me from my position. The wishy-washy words *might* and *maybe* also signal doubt. If the handyman is entertaining any doubt about what he's capable of, then guess what: I am going to doubt him too. And that means I am going to push until I am certain that the handyman has gone all the way to *his* resistance point. That means *I*, and not the handyman, will have succeeded in maximizing this deal.

Somewhere around is another doubt flag. Three hundred dollars is "somewhere around" $700, as is $400, $500, $600 and even $900. If the contractor leaves it open to pick a number "somewhere around" the proposed amount, then I am definitely going to choose a number that's around *my* target, not the handyman's. Language like this is a signal to a negotiator like me that the handyman can afford to go lower. Other similar flags would include *about*, *approximately*, *potentially* or *in the range of*. Any of those terms (and there are many others) that are placed ahead of the estimate make it seem less concrete and are an invitation to the other party to push harder for a better offer.

The handyman's proposal included one more signal that I should push for a lower price. Did you notice that he quoted a range? I have mixed emotions about ranges; they're helpful only in those circumstances where you feel like you need to work on the relationship and demonstrate some flexibility. Even then, you must choose your range strategically. Here, where the negotiation is focused solely on price and is unlikely to result in anything beyond a one-time transaction, a range is just a signal that the handyman is willing to accept less. Before you reply, "But what if he's trying to build a long-term relationship with you to come back and do more work?" I would tell you that offering a range is still not necessary. Even if he's coming to the home on a monthly basis (which is unlikely), he doesn't need to signal that he's overly flexible. That type of generosity may lead me to assume that I can get much lower rates out of him over the long term. Based on the signals the contractor is sending, I will consistently (though not maliciously) ask him to do more for less. (And remember, I have already ruled out the possibility of paying the low end of this supplier's range, let alone the higher end.)

If you are truly trying to build a long-term relationship, quoting a range occasionally won't do any harm, but by being more concrete and precise in your proposal, you also won't be doing any harm. Use your intuition, but when in doubt, just keep it simple. When you strip out all of those extra words that entice the other party to push back, we're left with: "For this project, it's $800."

Use the following principle when you're in any negotiation: *When in doubt, cut it out.* If you're unsure, there's no need to telegraph it to the other side. Say less, get more! No need to keep going on about it or explain anything further. State your price and then pause. In other words, *shut the hell up*! I can't think of any more short-and-sweet ways to express this point, but I think you get it. If you still don't, then I'd direct you to reread about my snow removal experience. People will talk themselves out of a good deal all the time. Your job as an effective negotiator is to listen for those clues instead of giving yourself away with soft language that signals doubt or movability. Be firm by being concise. This policy is especially important on the dark side.

Other examples of weak language include phrases like:

- **How about $X?** If you ask this, what would you expect them to say but no? If you offer your proposal in the form of a yes-or-no question, you don't exactly sound sure of yourself or signal that you're making a firm offer. Plus, it gives the other party an easy out to shoot you down.
- **I was hoping for/looking for/would have liked/ would be happy with . . .** I was hoping for a unicorn, but that doesn't mean I'm going to find it. And if it makes you instantly happy, then I think I've paid too much.
- **Let's split the difference.** We've talked about this one before. All it shows is that you've opened extreme enough to make meeting in the middle seem worthwhile. No thanks.

CHAPTER 27

MIND YOUR TONE

HUMOR, SARCASM, WARMTH, CONSTERNATION AND ANGER are things that can be misinterpreted in email and text messages, but are much more easily picked up in the sound of our voices. So, if you're trying to express any of these, you're better off getting away from the screen and speaking to someone live (or at least a recording)—bearing in mind that if you're not able to pause to keep your emotions in check, you may actually prefer to keep things in writing so that you don't say something that you'll regret.

There are plenty of benefits to using your voice. Humor is often a great way to defuse tension (assuming the timing and content are appropriate). If you're trying to convey how confident you are about your proposal, the tone of your voice can be a real asset. Anyone who is—or has had—a parent knows how effective a stern tone of voice can be. And when that parent slows down and pronounces every syllable of your name, you know they mean business and you're in trouble; "Fo-ti-NI" still sends shivers down my spine. And when you add the Greek accent to it? Watch out. A stern tone of voice combined with pacing that differs from your normal rhythm can signal a level of seriousness or gravity that kids are less likely to challenge than a more typical speech pattern.

Of course, with a more soothing voice, the slower pacing can actually have a different effect, one that can likely calm a room. FBI hostage negotiator Christopher Voss calls it his "late-night FM DJ voice." I don't recommend throwing your voice to some odd, inauthentic, different persona, but slowing down and turning down the volume a little can help to disarm people around you. Consider what happens when you're feeling super stressed or overstrung. Does someone screaming, "*CALM DOWN!! IT WILL BE FINE!*" help to ease your stress? Probably not. But if someone speaks to you in a soothing tone and tells you everything will be okay, or if you can hear that their breathing has slowed down as they speak slowly and deliberately, it may actually help to calm your nerves instead of getting you more riled up. Consider that context with little kids. Do they calm down when you scream at them to calm down, or do you need a different approach to take the edge off a tantrum?

A study on malpractice lawsuits for surgeons in the US found that those who were being sued were not necessarily the ones who were doing a bad job. In an article from *Cardiology Today*, "Malpractice claims against physicians are more likely when the physician fails to establish a trusting relationship with the patient." That's according to Professor Mohammadreza Hojat, who wrote the textbook *Empathy in Patient Care*. When surgeons were coached to adjust the way they spoke to patients, the number of lawsuits decreased. There is a massive benefit to pausing and being mindful about how you sound to those who are receiving your messages.

The sound of your voice can impact the way people engage with you, so it's worth considering how you sound to others, whether you've picked up any bad habits that may affect how you are perceived, and whether that drains your battery. Speaking like a monotonous robot, with no differences in pitch or rhythm, will make people tune you out. If you speak so quietly that people have a hard time catching everything you say, that will drain your battery by making others perceive that you lack confidence. This is certainly the case when I work with children—especially little girls—but I also see the same pattern in my MBA students when I have to ask them to speak up because I can't hear them. They start repeating their questions with the first word a little louder, and then fall right back into the barely audible voice.

When I first started training people on a daily basis, I found myself constantly dealing with laryngitis. I knew I was spending more time talking than I used to, but I was concerned that something bigger was wrong. I saw a specialist who inspected my vocal cords and said there was some inflammation—likely connected to my new working conditions, combined with some bad habits around sleep, food and hydration. She sent me to a speech pathologist who was going to help me optimize my habits to make my career sustainable. All sorts of machines measured the sound of my voice, and she found some strain when I was challenged to speak under conditions that simulated a large training room or a loud restaurant. She said that because I was speaking from the back of my throat instead of my diaphragm, I was putting extra stress on my cords. She suggested I speak in a higher register and add what I would describe as a melodic, singsongy voice—something you would envision when in a loud restaurant or bar. She asked if I could speak like that on a regular basis when I talked to clients, and I answered, "Uh, no." No one would take me seriously as a wise negotiation expert if I sounded like Snow White speaking to the seven dwarfs. Instead, we decided to spend our time on exercises to help me project from the diaphragm, as well as some massage techniques to release tension and strain from my jaw and throat.

On the flip side, I recall friends coming over to my house when we were kids and hearing my dad talk to any of us and thinking he was yelling. He wasn't. It was his natural voice. He also has hands the size of baseball gloves. When he whispers, it sounds like a normal speaking voice to the rest of us. You don't want him around when you're trying to put babies to sleep unless you're trying to train them to sleep around loud noises. My sister once bought him a T-shirt that says, "I'm not yelling. I'm Greek. This is how we talk." It's his favorite. He instills fear in quite a few people who are concerned about upsetting him further (it worked to his favor when he scared away boys who called our house). If you're someone who has a loud, booming voice, you want to be aware of the effect you're having on others. If you want to be perceived as more collaborative, you may need to make an extra effort to turn down the volume or slow your pace. It's not about being inauthentic; it's merely working in the most optimal place in the spectrum of your vocal capabilities.

BAD VERBAL HABITS TO AVOID

There are other tone issues to be aware of—in particular, tics that we tend to pick up from mirroring others, especially those we see on reality television shows. There's this thing? That sounds like a question? At the end of a phrase? That's actually a statement? Instead of a question? But it sounds like these question marks? Are inserted? In the middle of this sentence?

How annoying are those frequent question marks? It hurts my brain just to write them; it's even more painful to hear them. But that's what people often sound like when they're insecure about speaking. Imagine the handyman making his proposal with this upspeak inflection: "For this project? It's $800?" Is it, Mr. Handyman? Or is it a lot lower than that? When you want to express a firm proposal, make a statement, not a question, and make it *sound* like a statement, not a question.

I won't go into the epidemic of vocal fry (also known as creaky voice) that has leaked from reality TV into social discourse. That discussion is better saved for when you see me in person—I do a killer Kardashian impression. Just know this: the lackadaisical creakiness that comes with vocal fry is not a natural sound—I've looked this up—and it hurts your credibility. One of the most frequent questions I get from managers after my talks is: "How do I get the people on my team to stop doing the vocal fry thing you talked about?" My answer: go back to your authentic self and bring your best self forward, not the mannerisms you started mimicking from others around you.[9]

SPEAKING (AND LISTENING) IN
A NON-NATIVE LANGUAGE

For those who wonder about foreign-language accents, my advice is *don't sweat it*. If you are operating in your non-native language, kudos to you! You're probably executing a skill the other person isn't capable of, which should *boost* your confidence in the first place. Just take your time and articulate yourself well. If you're concerned that your messages aren't being understood, check in with the other party once in a while to make sure they're with you: "Is that clear? Should I repeat that?" As long as you don't have a condescending tone, you may actually be perceived as collaborative. When I conduct business in my second, third and fourth languages, I pause more than I've ever paused in my life. I find it works to my advantage because there's no way I'll ever go into autopilot, and it forces me to be much more considered about what I'm saying.

The first time I ran a workshop in Athens in Greek, I even went as far as managing expectations and stating up front that, although I'm familiar with the language, I'm not nearly as familiar with it as I am with English. I mentioned that I was sure they wouldn't appreciate me switching into English, so they would just need a little patience. I also offered that if I was being unclear, they should let me know. I wanted them to think that I must have had loads of confidence to step up in my non-native language—mentioning this fact was a technique I used to prevent them from draining my battery. It reminded them that I could, in fact, speak more than one language, which was more than most of them could do; that upped my credibility factor without making me seem arrogant. But by giving them the opening to speak up if they had trouble understanding me, what also happened was the creation of an environment of collaboration.

If you're speaking to someone with an accent that is different from yours, pause to consider the E test from their perspective. Where are they coming from (geographically and mentally)? Are they really doubtful, or is that the typical melody of their cultural norms? Inflection changes from culture to culture, so be aware before you jump to conclusions.

CHECK YOUR PACE

If you're aware that the other person is struggling to keep up with you, whatever the reason, give them time to absorb everything that you're saying. When I'm teaching a lecture and see a pen moving frantically across paper, I slow down because I want to make sure my audience is grasping everything I'm saying (I tend to speak ridiculously quickly—especially when I get passionate). The same is true when I'm in a negotiation. If you're about to drop a loaded proposal on them, one that's full of details and important information, take it slow so that they don't miss something—or worse, misinterpret something you said. You don't want to be assuming all is going well, only to find out that you're working with a total misunderstanding of who said what.

Pausing on the phone is even more important. You don't have the luxury of reading lips, expressions or gestures to piece together the entire message, so pausing becomes a necessity. But you also want to make sure that the other party isn't wondering whether the call was dropped because of some odd silence. My editor told me that when she's on the phone with *a new client, she tells them that if there's a long silence, that will be her, thinking—an excellent practice. You could also say* something like "I'll give you a chance to jot that down," "Let me think about that for a minute" or "I want to make sure I get that all down . . . just a second." Each of those phrases introduces the ability to pause without any awkwardness and signals to the other person that you are acknowledging them—a great way to build trust and collaboration.

When you've got the luxury of both words and tone, it reduces the chances of misinterpretation, which can obviously work to your advantage, but as I mentioned earlier, if you are someone who gets nervous easily, you may want to limit yourself to email/text/carrier pigeon. An alternative would be to channel your mental pause button to minimize the chances of your nerves taking over. Pause to take a breath. Be the one to make the phone call instead of waiting nervously to jump when the phone rings. PLAN! Write out what you want to say, and have it in front of you (on the phone, they won't be able to see that you have notes). Practice in advance so that when the words are coming out of your mouth for the first time, they're not coming out a jumbled mess.

I have a difficult name to pronounce (or so I'm told), and it can feel overwhelming for people. When all of that energy and attention go into just trying to say my name, it detracts from all the other things they want to say, and they start stumbling. At every event where I need to be introduced, I inevitably spend a minute with the host, listening to them practice my name. They usually get it right on the second try and a huge sigh of relief washes over them—the pause they need to focus on the other messages they want to communicate. Practice (or pausing) makes perfect.

CHAPTER 28

WITHOUT SAYING A WORD: MASTERING BODY LANGUAGE

WHEN MY NIECES WERE BORN, THEY WERE BIG BABIES and they were always hungry. When the first was born, and my exhausted sister was breastfeeding 24/7, I would visit as frequently as I could to play with the new little human and be of some assistance. The new baby was easygoing and rarely made a sound. But every once in a while when I was holding her, she'd have this angry look on her face and I'd flag it to my sister, who'd respond, "She's fine. She's just pooping." Lucky me. Other times, she'd start bobbing her head against my chest and slobbering on me. Turns out, she was looking for breast milk. You're not getting that from me, kid.

It was incredible to me that we started to learn her little messages. I mean, she'd whimper once in a while, and when she was pissed off or hungry (or both), she would show you what those lungs were made of, but usually we'd be able to decode her messages before she got to that point. That's the beauty of non-verbal communication. Facial expression and body language can tell us so much. But it wasn't foolproof. There were still times when we would be bewildered about what she was trying to say. She'd make these funny shapes with her mouth that freaked us out. Was she choking? About to laugh? About to cry? Or was she just trying to mirror what we were doing as we were cooing at her? If she had made a few sounds, it might have been easier to interpret without the stress of worrying that she was choking. Those babies like to keep you on your toes.

When I was a kid and my family was in church or at a restaurant, where we were expected to be on our best behavior, all my mom had to do was look at me with those eyes that opened a little wider than usual and a clenched jaw that screamed that I was going to be in trouble if I didn't smarten up. If she subtly extended her hand an inch with her palm facing me, it was a warning of a spanking (which didn't happen often, but this was a legitimate threat—it wasn't frowned upon back then). My dad had a similar look. He would point his chin down so his eyes were peeking out at you from under those giant eyebrows. Damn, that was intimidating. I'm told I have a look like that in the classroom when the class doesn't immediately settle down. I wonder if it was nature or nurture that gave me "the look." I did get it a lot (I liked to push boundaries), so I'm leaning toward nurture.

We can communicate so much without uttering a word. In negotiations, body language can be extremely valuable and immediately effective. When you're on the dark side of the spectrum, talking about price, and they put an extreme proposal on the table, what happens when you look at them with your jaw dropped and eyebrows raised? That look of surprise might rattle them into thinking that they've overestimated your resistance point and they've taken their proposal too far. When you look at them with a furrowed brow, they might assume you are angry about what they just said, and it may be time to back off of their extreme and move on to their next proposal. Meanwhile, you have yet to say a word. (There it is again: *Say Less, Get More!*)

I recall when a friend's toddler learned some colorful words that they didn't want him saying. When visiting, we were warned not to laugh when he did it, because that would merely encourage him to repeat the pattern. When that little person started dropping f-bombs his comedic timing was genius, but I had to pause to make sure I didn't burst into laughter. It was a moment that called for looking unimpressed, perhaps furrowing my brow along with the parents to reinforce the message that this was not to be repeated. When a group of you have consistent expressions on your faces, that is much more compelling than only one having a look of consternation while the others are smiling. Those mixed messages are confusing for the audience. If you go into a negotiation with a team and the other side makes a proposal that doesn't work for your group, but one of you is daydreaming and nodding their head enthusiastically, that inconsistent message won't exactly stop the other team dead in their tracks and force them to recalibrate the way you were hoping.

Too often in the business world, we're taught to be stoic, to never let them read your emotions. And I suppose that could be true to a degree. But I'd rather replace that lesson with encouraging you to choose the emotions you want other people to read. If I had been stoic with that toddler, he might have kept lobbing his comedic f-bombs until I finally started laughing. I wouldn't have been able to steer him off course. If I had been stoic instead of surprised when you proposed that extreme offer, you might have stopped making proposals, thinking, erroneously, that you must have offered me too good of a deal and you needed to slow down. When you slowed down, we would have gone from stoicism to deadlock and no deal. You would have been wondering what went wrong when everything seemed to be okay, or at least didn't look *not* okay.

What's the level of satisfaction going to be like if neither of you is willing to close a deal? What about if you decide that to avoid deadlock and close the deal, you make a jump to your resistance point? The other party should be happy, right? Wrong. They still think you're holding out on them and that there is more money to be had. It didn't look difficult or frustrating for you to give up that value, so why would they think otherwise? In a previous section, we talked about the size of your moves creating satisfaction, but the way you *communicate* that move (and your reaction to theirs) will also affect their satisfaction. Flip the *E* around to them to figure out what they need to feel satisfied. If they need to feel like they drove a hard bargain, then express the emotions that will help them believe that they did.

The way you show up, even before you start making proposals, also has an impact on the negotiation. You can charge or drain your battery before the negotiation begins. Take a moment to take inventory of your posture right now. Is your spine erect or is it curved? How about your shoulders? Are they curved forward or is your collarbone nice and wide? What about your neck—is it pitched forward as you look down or is it on top of your shoulders as you look forward? When you see that image in a mirror, does the person you

see look like someone who is ready to take on the world, or someone who looks defeated and about to take on more defeat? How do
you feel when you are in that slumped-over position? Are you ready
for success, or ready for a nap? What about if you sat up straight
or even stood up with your feet hip-width apart and your hands
on your hips like Wonder Woman or Superman? Superheroes are
always taking on what are called power poses. These are poses that
take up more space. Dr. Amy Cuddy made power poses famous in
her TED Talk, "Your Body Language May Shape Who You Are,"
and her book, *Presence*. There's the Wonder Woman, the Victor
(when you raise your hands in the air as though you've just crossed
a finish line), the CEO (hands wide and leaning on the podium or
table), the Villain (feet up on the desk and hands resting behind
your head) and the Manspread (if you've ever tried to sit in crowded
public transit, you know what I'm talking about).

Compare your hunched-over posture with the superhero:
Which looks more like a leader? Whose ideas or proposals are we
going to follow or push back on? Which looks more credible? The
more credible and confident you look, the more you charge your
battery and manage other people's perceptions. Go in there looking defeated, and your battery is already draining before you've
even started. Even when some of Dr. Cuddy's research was challenged, what was consistent in subsequent studies was that subjects
reported that they felt really good after holding a power pose for
two minutes.[10] I've come across plenty of research that indicates
that when you feel good or optimistic, you get better results. Go in
feeling pessimistic, and you'll become a self-fulfilling prophecy. So,
you do the math. Which posture is going to serve you best? How

do you want to show up? Taking up more physical space will help you manage perceptions—theirs and yours.

I think you get the point that body language can make a difference in how we're perceived, and there are a zillion fantastic books on the subject that go deep into detail (start with anything by Mark Bowden or Joe Navarro). Here are some key highlights that I would bear in mind as you have some of these difficult conversations.

Know your audience. Flip the *E* around and make sure you're aware of any perceptions or even cultural norms that will help or hurt you. For example, years ago when I was having dinner with extended family in Greece, I was engaged in conversation with someone at the table while a six-year-old was trying to get my attention to come see something at the other end of the table. I held my hand up and open to indicate I needed five minutes. This astute little fellow came over and explained, "Aunty, when you hold your hand up like that [palm open], it means a very bad word here [the equivalent of the middle finger or worse]. If you want to tell me you need five minutes, you need to turn your hand around and tell me this way" [and he showed me the back of his hand]. We both had a laugh at my gaffe. To this day I'm extremely conscious of doing anything with my palm open. My friends laugh when they see me hailing cabs with two fingers instead of an open palm, no matter what country I'm in. I do not need to make that mistake elsewhere. Familiarize yourself with customs to make sure you're not inadvertently sending messages you didn't mean to send.

Perceptions can change depending on your sex and general build. The same message may be perceived differently coming from you than from someone else. As a woman who's only five-foot-five, when I lean forward I may be perceived as someone who is interested or has something to add to the discussion. When my six-foot-four colleague is leaning forward, it could be perceived as an invasion of space or an intimidation tactic.

Along the same lines, make sure that you are aware of other people's personal boundaries. I'm not going to get into the physical contact that can get you into trouble. Pause to consider not how you prefer to greet people, but how others feel about physical contact, and avoid overstepping boundaries.

Also consider how you can create some boundaries by nudging people into mirroring your behavior. I was recently approached by a female executive who was seeking advice on how to handle people who wanted to greet her with a hug when she wasn't comfortable with it. Now that she was in a more visible role with a team that wasn't as closely knit as before, she didn't have the same comfort level and, frankly, didn't want to be hugged. My advice was to initiate the body language first. If you stick your hand out for a handshake first, you are anchoring what the communication should look like. Set the tone using your body language and they're more likely to follow suit. If that doesn't work, then you may have to supplement with some words: "I'm not much of a hugger," or "It's cold season and I don't want to take any risks." You don't need an excuse to keep someone from invading your personal space, but you don't want to embarrass them either. Flip the *E* around to figure out the best way to prevent them from going down that path.

Which seat do you take at the table? When you walk into a room, do you sit at the back of the room or the front? As a woman who is not very tall, if I sat at the back, I'd be jumping up and down to get someone to notice me and address my concerns in a room full of tall men. I want to make sure I can see and hear clearly, so I've always chosen a seat at the front. It turns out that people notice me more as well. I'm no wallflower. That's how I got my first consulting job, after all. One of my managers once told me that he knew he wanted to hire me as soon as I walked in the room. Now, before you jump to any gross conclusions, he said it was because I walked in wearing a red dress in a sea of men in dark golf shirts and looked like I owned the joint. I was projecting confidence and credibility; that told him he needed to know more about me.

How you decide to dress can have an impact on how people perceive you. Are you looking polished or like a slob? Are you wearing a power suit in a room full of techies who are wearing jeans and sneakers? How do you think people will receive you? If you're trying to build trust, you may want to adjust your wardrobe to seem more approachable. Or maybe you want them to take you as seriously as possible, and the suit will create that impression from the get-go. Pause to consider the circumstances and the best outcomes.

Are you going into a competitive situation or a collaborative one? You may wish to consider whether you want to sit across the table from someone, in what could be perceived as an adversarial position, or sit perpendicular to them to present a more collaborative approach.

Do you want to be in "tell it like it is" mode, or do you want to get them to open up? The look on your face will affect that. A sterner look may create the firm messaging you need in the "me" side of negotiation, whereas you may want to express some warmth by relaxing your face if you want to get them to open up to you on the "we" side.

Consider how you talk to kids. Do you want to be standing and looking down at them when you're giving them serious orders, or do you want to kneel down to their level to have a discourse with them that encourages understanding? Pause to think about what you're trying to accomplish and the best placement to get that result.

When you're on the lighter side of the negotiation spectrum (and even sometimes on the dark side), the temptation may be to nod your head or tilt it to one side to demonstrate that you are listening. The problem is that these moves are likely to be perceived as agreement or submission. There are other ways to acknowledge that you're listening, perhaps by squinting your eyes as if you're trying to understand or leaning forward to show some interest. Pause to decide how each gesture will be perceived. The bobblehead approach is usually the most common and most dangerous involuntary reaction I see.

If you want to emit an open and trustworthy vibe, consider what your hands are doing. You may be comfortable with them folded across your chest, but that can make you look closed off. That may work in your favor on the dark side, but if you want to create trust, you could keep your hands near your belly button with your palms open, which conveys that you have nothing to hide.

Taking notes is a great way to demonstrate that you are listening and a best practice to make sure that you've got a good recollection of what went down, but be careful of burying yourself in notes. Look up from time to time, or you might be perceived as the eager beaver; more importantly, you might miss out on important cues that the other party is giving you. If you're looking down the whole time, you may not see the firmness or flexibility on their faces as they relay a proposal to you. If you need to get them to repeat what they said, do it. Better to do that than miss some important messages.

There is a ton of research on things like eye contact (or lack thereof), fidgeting, postural shifting, face touching, blinking and more. Here's the thing: not only is there often conflicting data, but you, a layperson who doesn't have the luxury of slow-motion video in the moment, are unlikely to be able to assess what that means. We are not very good human lie detectors. But that doesn't mean you should dismiss everything you might see. The key is to look at the big picture and watch for inconsistencies. Did otherwise calm people get fidgety when you asked a question on a particular subject? It's that change in behavior that is more noteworthy than the behavior itself. If they do a couple of things like avoiding eye contact or tapping their pen incessantly, some may jump to the conclusion that they are lying. In fact, the odds are they are nervous; the question is why? Maybe they just suck at conflict. Maybe they get nervous around new people. Anyway, there's a good chance they aren't lying. Take in the context as well as the body language before you jump to any conclusions.

CHAPTER 29

SCRIPTS THAT WORK

AS WE'VE ESTABLISHED, EMOTIONS OFTEN RUN HIGH IN negotiations, so it's tempting to lash out at the other person. A study that compared expert negotiators with average ones[11] found that average negotiators (who got suboptimal results) were more likely to use defend/attack spirals, emotionally charged statements that lead to a series of reciprocal emotional statements from the other party, such as:

- "You can't blame us for that," or
- "Oh yeah? Well, let me tell you something . . ."

If you use these statements, you'll trigger the other party to get upset, which will escalate the situation further, and you might end up going down some rabbit hole of all the reasons why your viewpoint is better than theirs. Here's the thing: they don't care. They care about *their E, their Why, their* perspective, and when you try to shove yours down their throat, they're just going to want to dig their heels in further and continue arguing with you. I see this happening more often on what should be the more collaborative side of the spectrum, where we're supposed to be looking for mutual interest or a common Why.

WHAT TO DO INSTEAD

What to do instead of getting caught up in these little traps? *PAUSE.* After that, here are some firm words you can say when you don't like their proposal:

- "You're going to have to do much better than that." (Appropriate for the dark side negotiations.)
- "I can't come close to that . . ." [*Pause.*] "Here's what I *can* do." (Appropriate for the dark side, but also useful heading into the lighter side—focus on what you *can* do instead of what you *can't* do.)
- "How close can you get to my figure?" (This will pull them to make a counterproposal close to your figure instead of staying at some undesirable anchor.)
- When you hear "I can't," answer with "How could you . . ." or "Under what circumstances . . . "
- Instead of pointing out, "We're so far apart," try telling them, "Here's what needs to happen to get to a deal."
- "Why is that?" (Used when you're deep into probing. Find out the *real* problem. This is particularly useful on the lighter side but can also be helpful to get them to give themselves away on the dark side. Beware,

though; later in this chapter, we'll discuss how other uses of *why* can get you into trouble.)

- And when you're getting even more collaborative: "I have an idea that could help us [insert a reference to a common Why]. I propose we do this . . . "

USING QUESTIONS WELL

In the same study of expert and average negotiators, researchers compared how often negotiators asked questions. Expert negotiators asked nearly three times as many questions per hour as average ones. Why?

Questions are a great way to get information, and we know how powerful information can be to charge our batteries. We get a better understanding of their Why and what their *E* means by asking questions.

Questions are your best tool for assessing whether people are lying to you. Ask a question you already know the answer to, or ask multiple questions that will help you triangulate the truth.

Questions are an obvious way to demonstrate that you are listening (and to force yourself to listen). You can't ask an intelligent, probing question if you're not paying attention to what they just said.

Questions are also one of the most effective ways to manage conflict instead of ending up in a boxing match. If the conversation feels like it's coming to a standstill with no resolution in sight, you can get it going again by asking a question. If it feels like it's getting adversarial, use your questions to bring it back to a Why that will resonate. Christopher Voss refers to questions like these as *calibrated questions*. Here are some examples:

- What's the objective? What problem are we trying to solve? Get them to rearticulate the Why, and they'll feel more compelled to fulfill it.
- What are your biggest obstacles? Demonstrate concern for their challenges, assuming you've built enough trust to get them to open up.
- How would this solve the problem? If they're getting hung up on a proposal, dig a little deeper to figure out their interest instead of getting stuck at the proposal.
- How can we make this better for everyone? Notice it's *we*, not *you*, because this is to be mutually beneficial. It's not about pandering to them; you need to take care of both *E*s. Using *we* puts some of the onus on them, instead of letting them assume you need to take all of the responsibility.
- What can we do from here? You might prompt them to come up with a solution—or, at a minimum, understand what's holding up the next step in this deal.
- How did we get here? Do you truly understand the source of the problem and the interest you're solving for?

We're often tempted to go into "telling" mode and give the other party directions on what to do. That rarely goes over well when things are already heated or they have a big ego (or both).

Instead of saying, "That's never going to work; this is what we need to do," you can handle the situation in a less combative way by saying, "I'm not quite seeing how this will work out. What do you think about this option?" This version isn't quite as directive, and uses a question to prompt the other party to speak. By getting their feedback, you could collect some valuable information on why they're resisting, and in the process, you'll be engaging them in the creation of the direction, which will make them feel more accountable to it. If they can't come up with a viable reason the option doesn't work, they'd look foolish not to go along with it.

Instead of saying, "The boss [or client] will never go for that," you could use a question to make their ego feel less bruised. "How do you think the boss will respond to this direction?" The question format forces them to think about the consequences without the resistance that comes with your *telling* them the consequences. Whether they say it out loud or just in their head, they'll be more compelled to follow the thought process that was theirs instead of the one you specified for them.

A photographer recently shot a lecture where I gave this example. She told me afterward, "That's how I talk to my husband all the time. Just yesterday, he posted something on social media that I thought was in poor taste. Instead of telling him that I thought it was poor judgment or telling him to take it down, I asked, 'What prompted you to post that? What do you think your friends and colleagues will make of it?' He responded with 'You know what? Maybe it's not such a good idea' and took it down." This example could easily be replicated with children to help them to gain some understanding of their choices, instead of constantly telling them what to do and having them rebel against you.

Instead of telling someone that they're being ridiculous for making an absurd demand and sparking an all-out war with them, you could ask something straight out of the FBI hostage negotiator's handbook: "How am I supposed to do that?" By avoiding the "tell" mode, you're prompting them to pause to think about their demand. To preserve their ego, they may say, "I don't know; that's your problem." But the impression has been made. Deep in their subconscious, you've planted some seeds of doubt and insecurity about their proposal, which will increase the likelihood of their accepting a less extreme proposal without hurting your credibility. Best-case scenario: they answer by retracting their proposal and putting something less extreme on the table. Either way, you'll have influenced them to back off in some way without inflaming them further.

A word of caution: If you are asking, "How am I supposed to do that?" via email or text message, be aware that the tone could easily be misinterpreted as aggressive and could make things worse. If you use it on the phone or in person, you need to pause to be mindful of how you ask it. Where you put the emphasis matters. "How am I supposed to do that?" in a matter-of-fact, measured tone is different from "How am *I* supposed to do that?" or "How am I supposed to do *that*?" which sounds combative, as if to say, "What are you—an idiot?" Tone still matters.

WHY NOT "WHY"?

You'll notice two characteristics about these questions I've been listing. The first is that the word *why* is missing. Studies show us that people get defensive when you ask them "why" questions. Don't believe me? Go home and ask your partner, "Why did you do that?" and they'll likely retort, "Why are you attacking me?" True story. Yet "why" has been such an important theme in negotiation, so what is one to do? How about a tiny modification: replace your *why* with *what* or *how*. Instead of "Why did you do that?" try "What caused you to do that?" or "How did you come to that?" Both of those questions will uncover the why without the defensive behavior. They provide the path of least resistance to get to the bottom of things.

These open-ended "how" and "what" questions also lead to more open answers than closed, yes-or-no questions. If you give someone competitive the opportunity to say no, they will take it. "Can we do it this way?" No. "Do you want to do it this way?" No. Switch it up to a question framed by *how* or *what*, and you're likely to get a more informative, collaborative response, just as we did above.

When I hear the words *no* or *I can't*, my automatic response is to ask, "How could you . . ." or "What circumstances would it take to get there?" *No* is just the start of the negotiation when you've got questions ready; it doesn't have to be the end.

PAUSE FOR REFLECTION

SECTION 6 | COMMUNICATE LIKE A PRO
CHECKLIST OF KEY TAKEAWAYS

✓ **Start with mindset.** Effective communication begins with mindset and self-control. Practice will help you access your pause button in the moment.

✓ **Be mindful of the three modes of communication.** We communicate using our words, our tone and our body language. When we don't have the luxury of all three, there is a risk of misinterpretation. When the modes are in conflict, body language dominates our interpretation.

✓ **Warm up.** Spend a little extra time creating a warm climate before you make that proposal via email or text. But always pause to choose your words carefully. Less is usually more when it comes to making proposals.

✓ **Tone matters.** Your tone of voice can affect your credibility and affect how others respond to you. Don't be afraid to pause and to slow. It. Down.

✓ **Pose like a pro.** Instead of being stoic, choose the emotions you want them to read on your face and in your body language. Pause to practice a power pose to get yourself ready!

- ✓ **Choose your words wisely.** Experts and average negotiators communicate differently. Avoid phrases that can cause conflict and follow some of the scripts that work!
- ✓ **Ask questions.** Experts ask nearly three times as many questions as average negotiators. Get some knowledge and manage conflict with some effective questions. But phrase your "why" questions as "what" or "how" questions to avoid eliciting defensive behavior.

EPILOGUE

NOW WHAT? NEGOTIATION IN ACTION

WHEN I TAKE ON A SEMESTER OF TEACHING, MY MBA students have twelve weeks to practice finding their way across the spectrum and to get used to seeing the signals that guide them toward appropriate strategies and behaviors. At the end of the semester, they have to write a paper reflecting on what they've learned and how they've changed as negotiators. The truth is, I don't really care how they performed during the semester, and their grade is not at all dependent on how successful their negotiations were. It *is* dependent on what they learned from their mistakes (or successes—but mostly mistakes) along the way. The largest part of their grade is weighted to this single assignment, where they recall what stood out for them and what they're going to do as a result.

They even get a bonus mark for sharing an action plan with me. It's what happens when they *leave* my class that is going to have the biggest impact for years to come, and I would hate to have twelve weeks of work go out the window when they walk out of my classroom. Reading these papers is my favorite part of the semester. I get excited reading about the confidence they've found, the success

stories they take pride in sharing, and which pieces of content reso-
nated. These papers have been informing my keynote speeches and
have been a fantastic way to identify the most valuable insights that
created this book.

Of the hundreds of papers I've read over the years, one stuck out
the most. It brought tears to my eyes and demonstrated how being
able to identify different types of negotiation can be life-changing.

NEGOTIATION LENS CREATES LIFE-CHANGING RESULTS

Layla is a young, bright and somewhat reserved woman with a ton
of potential ahead of her. She always sat in the front row with a
quiet confidence. She began her paper by telling me about some
unfortunate and violent circumstances in her life that started in her
childhood. It was gripping, but I had no clue what it had to do with
negotiation and, more specifically, my class. And then she continued to describe her aha moment about *me* and *we* negotiations:

> One Monday afternoon Fotini drew a line on the board
> with the word competitive on one end and the word col-
> laborative on the other end. She said that "sometimes in
> life, even if we're naturally here," she said, circling the word
> collaborative, "we need to recognize the negotiation for
> what it is and move our approach to here," she said, circling
> the word competitive. Those who are naturally inclined
> to competitive negotiations can easily take advantage
> of someone who tries to compromise, and those who are

naturally inclined to be collaborative need to think about how they're meeting their own needs. I don't know what it was about that moment but suddenly, it all clicked for me. I was choosing relationships with people who are naturally competitive value claimers but still actively seeking out collaborative interactions, giving more of myself than was fair, simply because I thought that was my role. I was creating complexity and pouring trust into relationships that were essentially zero-sum, where the other party could only gain calm or emotional stability at the expense of my energy and time. I began to examine the recent interactions I had had with my partner; how abusive they had really been without me even realizing it. How I had made concessions and allowed him to claim value because I went into the relationship with the intent to compromise on my safety when really, that should always have been my walk-away point. Writing it out this way feels a bit inauthentic, as if there's a textbook explanation for situations that aren't black and white. But the truth is, we learned in class that collaborative conflict styles are inappropriate when immediate decisions are required. And taking a step to securing my own safety is a decision that needed to be taken immediately.

In our last class, Fotini summarized this piece of knowledge by explaining the importance of pausing to reevaluate your approach to find where you should really position yourself, in spite of your instincts [to react to the stimulus]. I've always known this to be true for other people, especially for those with violent, aggressive or manipulative *tendencies, but I had never thought about how it could be true for me. No, I'm not naturally inclined toward violence or manipulative tactics, but I too am guilty of taking the wrong approach. If I recognize that my tendency is to be patient, calm and understanding of someone's destructive tendencies, I need to pause and re-evaluate the outcomes of using such an approach. Usually, the result of my collaborative approach is that I remain stuck in an undesirable situation because I feel that it's my job to find holistic and creative solutions when really, I may not even need to be at the table. It's important for me to pause and reflect on my approach. This is something that was reinforced in different ways throughout the course.*

When taking an interests-based approach, my focus was primarily on the other party's interests without fully considering my own. Now I feel that I am more likely to pause and ask myself if I am ensuring that my voice and interests are heard and represented in this dispute. I intend to ask myself if I am putting myself at risk by continuing to engage and how I will feel when the dispute is resolved in this way. The likelihood of recurrence is also an important factor in my decision-making now.

There are so many lessons packed into this one excerpt. Most imperative, Layla learned that identifying the type of negotiation situation you're facing can help to identify the potential outcomes. She realized that she was hoping to get collaborative results from a competitive negotiator who was consistently demonstrating "taker" or My Way behavior time and again. Whether it was her time, attention or love that was treated as a scarce commodity, her partner wanted all of it. And she wasn't getting what she needed in return, thus the imbalance of a My Way negotiation.

Negotiation is not about wishful thinking. It's about using your analytical and observational skills to identify where the opportunity for the best results lies. In Layla's situation there were no collaborative results to be had; just someone who was repeatedly trying to take whatever they could. Over time, this included her safety and well-being. She acknowledged this by continuing:

> In class, we learned how important it is to establish boundaries, defining them as our resistance points. For my personal situation, I need to view my resistance point as the place where I feel I'm at risk, I'm being treated unfairly or where staying in the relationship, or "negotiation," would do more harm than if I were to walk away.

I'm happy to report that just before the end of the semester, as she was writing this paper, she moved out of the home she shared with her partner and set new boundaries to live by. My hope for Layla is that she will continue to pause to use her negotiation skills and foresight to identify this type of conflict sooner and without turmoil. I hope she continues to feel empowered to take on the challenges that come her way instead of allowing My Way negotiators to take advantage of her collaborative nature. At the time of writing, she has completed her degree and is doing well.

When I hear these stories from my students, clients and even strangers who have sat in audiences or on the other side of a podcast, I'm amazed at what changes can take place because of some tiny adjustments in mindset, strategy or both. Whether they entail a pause to take a breath or spending a few minutes to prepare a move plan, these little actions can go a long way.

REVISITING THE SPECTRUM TO INCREASE VALUE

Over the course of this book we have covered a lot of principles that can help you to identify new ways to get what you want. Being able to identify the type of negotiation, whether it's a My Way or an Our Way, will help you to plan the best approach to maximize your results. Pausing to make sure you identify all of the opportunities will unlock all sorts of value. If you don't believe me, take it from one of my students who shared this:

> I'm in the process of interviewing with a bank, and when the recruiter called me to discuss salary, I gave her my number. The funny thing is that because of you, I have started to not just focus on the salary figure but also consider negotiating the other aspects of the offer as well (vacation, bonus, stock payout, etc.). It really took me back to that job-offer discussion in class. I have learned to look at negotiations from a holistic perspective. If they cannot offer me my salary, what else can they give me? Will they give me more vacation time? More money in stocks? Better benefits? The perspective has given me so much leverage and confidence

to push for what I truly deserve. It's not always about the salary.

The other thing I have learned from you is that if they cannot offer me the salary now, how can I prepare myself to negotiate and push for that number again in the future when I'm asking for a raise? How can I arm myself? I have learned to log my projects to show a story on why I deserve that raise. Thank YOU for that! I was thinking about you during the whole process. Granted, I have not received the offer yet, but you best believe that I will be negotiating. I'm not afraid to ask anymore!

EXPRESSING YOUR POWER TO INCREASE RESULTS

Power is another area where we have focused on identifying what charges or drains your battery. Pausing to consider how much power you have when you go in to negotiate will set you up with an attitude for success. And power doesn't come from being aggressive; it comes from confidence and owning what you bring to the table. This was nicely summed up by one audience member:

I used to think negotiation was a lot of fist-pounding in movies . . . men yelling at each other to get what they want. After previously experiencing being lowballed and underpaid as a freelancer, I am much better at negotiating for what I want. It is about asserting myself, and not being afraid to ask. Often, I have learned that clients are willing to give me what I want if I can justify my professionalism and expertise with confidence. I have also noticed that people treat me with more respect. I've realized that being respected is more important than being liked by others.

LEARNING MORE ABOUT THE PEOPLE TO GET OVER OBSTACLES

Of course, we need to pause to consider the people involved in the negotiation: you *and* the person on the other side of the table. I learned the hard way that what works for one person may not work for someone else. Identify your interests and spend some time thinking about what's going on inside their brain to determine how to get them to do what you need, as this audience member did:

I've always been uncomfortable in negotiations. It came from a fear of losing out on what I wanted. I'd rather pay a higher amount or acquiesce a bit in order to make people comfortable. Your session reset that thought process for me. While I don't negotiate price in my business, there is a nego-tiation with the client all the time. As a fiduciary, I have to do what's best for the client by law and I always put my best recommendation forth. However, clients don't always want to do what's best for various reasons, and when they don't it's really my fault in terms of lack of communication. It doesn't happen all the time, but the few times it does I consider it that I've failed them. I've used your language and your pauses to great effect. I've bettered my questions and I've incorporated them in a more effective way, and I've been able to help and serve more people.

CREATING A PROCESS TO ACHIEVE SUCCESS

Even when you've considered all of the psychology around why and how people do what they do, you still need a process to create a road map to success. One conference attendee shared this story about how preparation helped her get out of a rut:

> *I heard you speak a few years back. I was working full time at the same charity for about a year and a half at that point and felt I was being underpaid, and my title did not reflect the level of work and responsibility I was taking on and executing fully. I was frustrated and admittedly very full of self-pity . . . aka, not in a productive mindset. Your talk gave me the wakeup call that I needed to build a plan: stop complaining and start setting myself up to get the promotion I wanted.*
>
> *Here's what I did (and continue to do)—all inspired by your talk:*
>
> 1. *I did a ton of research on salaries for not only my job title, but also the job titles that reflected the type of work I was actually doing. My manager at the time kept saying I was the highest-paid with my title (as a reason to justify my salary), so I wanted to reframe the discussion with new market benchmarks.*
>
> 2. *I also wanted to shift the conversation to my contribution and what impact I was having on the team.*

I created a spreadsheet outlining my achieved performance on the skills and responsibilities expected for my current level and all of the special initiatives I had taken on in addition. I then framed my ask around what new responsibilities and initiatives I would like to take on, and how it would help with the team's overall objectives. (When I shared this with my current director, she said, "Wow. This is amazing. I wish everyone would take the initiative and do this!")

3. *I was bold with my ask and advocated for myself consistently. The stat you shared about how many more years women would have to work because they don't negotiate their first job offer really made me pissed off. I knew I was in that boat. And I wanted to get out of it, pronto.*

And it all worked! I got my first promotion a year ago. When it was announced, many of my team members (most of whom had been there longer than me) asked how I got the promotion. They were happy for me but wondered why they weren't considered. I said I built a case and asked persistently. They simply had not ever asked. Or passingly asked once a year.

I am currently in the final stages of negotiating another promotion—this time I had to make a case for a whole new role to be made. It was an even bolder ask. I used the same approach—research, build a case for how I can help the team achieve its goals and metrics even further in a more leadership role, and be persistent in asking for feedback and checking in if I'm on track for my "plan." I am of course lucky to have a supportive boss who responds well to this approach. She's a rock star and is such a role model for me in the kind of leader I want to be some day.

You lit a fire inside me during that talk that has persisted. It's been a total mind shift. For me, it's now about knowing my worth and not being shy or humble about it to myself (aka, actually believing it), which has helped me speak more confidently when advocating to my director.

With 9 percent increases at both promotions, I am certainly getting there. But it meant I had to set bold targets that aligned with the team objectives, put the stake in the ground and communicate it to my director, and then work my ass off to get there.

COMMUNICATING CAREFULLY TO GET WHAT YOU WANT

When you've got a bold plan ready to go, you still need to pause to think carefully about how you're going to communicate this proposal, whether via an email, phone call or live conversation. The *way* we get our messages across is critical to our success. A workshop client recently shared how he put this into action:

Since the new year I've been taking on more ownership of negotiating with our sales team internally on things like *discounts to our service offerings, timelines we can commit to, customer projects, etc. I've been coming back to the "if you . . . then I" structure a lot and have found it to be very useful! As an example: "If you can give me the new solutions engineer you're onboarding for a week to support a project and offset my costs, then I can give you $5,000 off the services for the implementation." I've found it to be much more successful at getting everyone to a happy outcome than treating each negotiation as bargaining or a conflict.*

Of course, the language is just as valuable outside of the office, as demonstrated by someone who messaged me right after a talk and shared, "I used 'if you . . . then I' with my two-year-old yesterday, and it worked!"

PAUSING YOUR MIND TO ACKNOWLEDGE YOUR WORTH

I get so many wonderful messages from people who are eager to share their success stories with me, and I never tire of hearing them. The one thing they have in common is that the moment they walked away from the speech, classroom or webinar, they all started shifting their mindset to find value right away. That's your next step. Picking up this book is just the beginning of your transformation. Take it from one audience member who attended a fifteen-minute talk I did last year:

The story you shared about the importance of negotiating your salary was eye-opening. Retiring years earlier because of negotiation skills? Sign me up! The pause button is also a wonderful tool. Now when I'm in a situation, I click the pause button and I think: "Is there some room for negotiation here?" The irony of it all is that my dad is an entrepreneur and a great negotiator, but I never really paid attention. When you presented the stats, it lit up a bulb in my mind. I have a boutique that curates one of a kind ethnic Indian/Pakistani and Tanzanian clothing (including bridal). I can't tell you how many projects I took where I didn't compensate myself enough for the amount of work I was putting in. If I get a bridal order, I'm up at 5 a.m. every morning, speaking with designers in India. However, I'm happy to report I compensated myself adequately on all of my orders since last week, THREE YEARS into my business.

One week of orders leads to another year's worth, followed by an early retirement. Pressing that pause button will also lead to reduced stress levels and higher quality of life, as it did for this attendee:

I have the pause button all over my house and in my wallet as reminders when my anxiety is high. I have also found the visual helps with coaching clients! The visual of seeing a pause button and taking a breather has worked wonders for me.

A simple shift in your mindset around getting what you want can be life-altering, as it was for this person:

> HUGE aha moment: shifted from fearing (white, wealthy, aggressive, male) C-suite execs to boldly showing how much I can do to make their life easier—and really owning my expertise. Plus, they go wild for methodical strategic plans and metrics. I'm going to earn so much more with this mindset!

This is what you are capable of achieving when you start putting this into practice. Failing is okay—do it in lots of low-stakes negotiations. That's what kids do, and they're fantastic at it! Imagine how much better you can be now that you know how to access your pause button.

WHAT ABOUT WHEN YOU DON'T GET WHAT YOU SET OUT TO ACHIEVE?

"Are you happy now?" he asked as he gave me a smug look. I'll never forget that moment, even though it seems like ages ago. I was at a sales conference in the Caribbean with my former employer. I had just been promoted and had confronted my HR representative about a salary issue related to my new assignment. I should share that I had previously negotiated a salary increase at this same workplace as part of a promotion (even before I became a negotiation consultant), and I planned to use the same strategy here: a civil conversation full of questions and cooperative behavior.

I even had the knowledge that the company *could* pay more because I had just found my predecessor's old contract, left carelessly on the photocopier, so I was expecting a salary comparable to hers. We had the same amount of work experience and she was known to make mistakes, so I'd had the responsibility of checking her work before it went to the client. There were also some power dynamics working in my favor because my taking the promotion triggered a domino effect for three other people who were going to shift roles. If I delayed this process, it would affect all of those subsequent moves, and HR wanted to have everything sorted out before the weekend, when we were headed off to the Caribbean.

Even with all of these factors in my favor, the salary offer fell significantly short of my predecessor's compensation—and I was the one who had been correcting her mistakes! It was the end of the day on Thursday when I spoke with the HR rep who had presented my offer. When it wasn't greeted with a burst of joy—my response was a delayed, hesitant "okayyy . . ."—she asked what was wrong. I told her I was "surprised" (I chose my words carefully so as not to insult anyone) to see that the offer wasn't as high as I expected, especially as I had received larger increases when moving up from previous roles. She told me she personally couldn't do anything about the offer, but she would talk to her boss and promised to get back to me with some information the following morning. I thanked her and we ended cordially.

I thought it was a pleasant conversation. I relayed the details to a colleague who had coached me through the negotiation (the highest-paid manager in the group, who seemed to know what he was doing) and he agreed it sounded positive.

I never heard back from the HR rep. Instead, first thing in the morning, I got a call from my manager's manager (the vice-president of my division), telling me *he* had received a call from the VP of human resources, who told him he was ready to fire this ungrateful employee he had heard about. Whoa—that escalated quickly! My VP asked why I was so curt in demanding more money. *What?!* That wasn't what had gone down. The HR rep had offered to take it up before I even had a chance to make a counterproposal.

My boss's boss was shocked when I gave him the recap, followed by "Do you really think I would say anything that stupid?" Fortunately, he didn't. He also thought it was odd, which is why he told HR he would sort things out. We determined that there was not going to be any change to my offer (duh) and that we needed to do some damage control. He would tell them I was happy to take the offer as it stood, and he advised me that when I saw the VP of HR at the hotel, I should politely smile and nod to rectify the situation—the equivalent of groveling for forgiveness for challenging the king.

I felt sick to my stomach. Some game of broken telephone and some fragile egos were conspiring to keep me earning less money than I deserved? No way.

I didn't get what I wanted in that negotiation. But I got something much better: the confirmation that it was time to go (and a fun last hurrah in the Caribbean with my work friends). I had discovered my resistance point. It was time to explore my BATNAs, which led me to a job with a much higher salary and way fewer work hours!

My most memorable negotiation wasn't my most fruitful, but it was the most life-changing. A colleague was complaining to me about his latest salary increase. I was happy to lend a supportive ear, but in the process, I learned that his disappointing increase was bigger than mine! This despite my greater experience, seniority and quantitative results. I was livid. I knew our boss had played favorites (spoiler: the favorite was not me, despite my positive evaluations), but this was ridiculous.

I set up a meeting with my boss to discuss the matter. I prepared. I had questions ready. I had done some internal research and I had data ready. And I was prepared to implement all of my negotiation skills. So, I raised the issue, but not surprisingly, the conversation escalated quickly. I was accused of not bringing in the same results as my peer. I had the emails and data to dispute those claims, showing I had brought in more. When he was backed into a corner with no excuses left, he started lying. Telling me about how he had stuck his neck out for me, along with some other clichés about what a wonderful manager he was (he wasn't, he had no examples to support his claims, and he was eventually relieved of his management role). If there's one way to get under my skin, it's lying to me. I see red. And just as my blood had started boiling and my voice started getting louder, I paused. I had this out-of-body experience. I was watching this all go down and I realized that the more I said, the more ammunition I would give him to call me emotional—a trait that wasn't well received in that business. I would only end up giving him the excuses he needed to put me in a category that wasn't as shiny and bright as his favorite employees, which would justify his discriminatory pay scale.

Nope. I wasn't going to do it. I wasn't going to hand that to him. I was going to come out shining and rational. Say less, get more. I paused to let all of these thoughts go through my mind and I said, "Thank you." I've never seen a more confused look on someone's face. I thought my video screen had frozen. I clarified, "If you're telling me you stuck your neck out for me, then thank you." He looked a little relieved. As though he had gotten away with it . . . until . . .

"I'll take it from here," I told him. "If you've done everything you can, then I'll take it from here. I wouldn't be able to sleep at night knowing I haven't done everything I can to rectify it."

That's when the look of panic came over his face. "I don't think you should raise this with HR or [my boss]." This confirmed exactly what I suspected: he had done nothing for me. His personal bias and ego were driving this decision.

I'll spare you some of the sordid details because I've made my point. But I'll fast-forward to tell you that I did raise it with his boss, and that conversation went similarly: it started with lies. But instead of letting my heated Mediterranean blood take over and losing my temper, I paused. I had that out-of-body experience again and asked a series of questions that forced him to get caught in his lies and expose himself. It was so satisfying. And yet there was no way I was going to rectify this salary issue. Even after a second attempt. Once again, my negotiation outcome wasn't what I set out to achieve. But what I got was so much more valuable. I proved to myself that I was working with people who were never going to acknowledge my worth and no longer shared my values. It confirmed my suspicions *and* that I had hit my breaking point. This negotiation provided all the validation I needed to take my next step: out the door. And I did. I left that company, and it felt amazing.

I'm not sure I'd feel so great about this situation if I hadn't been so well prepared or paused to execute so meticulously. I might not have felt so confident about the outcome. I might not have left.

Sometimes you just can't change minds or people. Sometimes, despite your best efforts, even when you've done everything by the book, you just don't make it over the finish line. Sometimes it's because they really didn't have the budget. Other times, some information you weren't privy to wasn't factored into your strategy. And sometimes it just comes down to people being ruled by their irrational emotions or biases and you just can't change them—not even the best therapists can crack those nuts.

There are always variables that are beyond your control that can affect your outcome. And when that happens, you could beat yourself up and consider yourself a failure. (I've been there.) Or you can use it as a jumping-off point to realize your worth and seek out the conditions that will meet them. I know it's not always easy to do overnight, but having that glimmer of hope that there is something better out there—and that you can invest your energy in finding it—makes getting through the day a lot easier. It also builds confidence. Among the hundreds of messages I get that document success stories, there's always an occasional note to tell me that someone who made the effort didn't achieve their desired result. But even that one is always accompanied by a story of how they feel so much more confident and prepared to advocate for themselves, carry themselves with credibility and look forward to the next opportunity. That one negotiation may be a lost battle, but it's one step closer to winning the war. Every time you stand up for yourself, you'll appear a little taller, both to yourself and to others. And that feels freaking amazing.

Knowing how to stand up for yourself is one of the greatest lessons you can learn, and I hope that is your greatest takeaway from this book. Negotiation is about more than money. It's about self-worth.

YOUR FINAL ASSIGNMENT

I'm pulling out my teacher card one last time for you. A few weeks from now (or less), how do you want to describe yourself as a negotiator? What habits do you hope will be different from today? As soon as you finish reading, what action plan will you put in place to make that a reality? How can you engage your friends and colleagues in discussion about this book to keep the lessons top of mind? When will you start planning for your next salary increase? That new car? That coworker who's been driving you nuts? As we draw to a close, consider the following questions:

> What am I leaving on the table in my life?
> What's holding me back from getting what I want?
> Which of the tools in this book will help me get there?
> Who can I lean on for support?

My eyes water every time I read Layla's story, and I have a smile on my face every time I get one of these messages. Maybe your moment won't be as big as Layla's story or some of the others you've read here. But as long as it's something that brings you satisfaction and lets you walk away feeling proud of yourself, you have achieved your objective. I know that if you have made it this far, you too are going to be capable of such incredible things and be a role model for others around you as an empowered person who can take on whatever challenges come their way. I only hope that you reach out to share your stories with me, because I can't wait to hear them!

ACKNOWLEDGMENTS

GETTING TO THIS PAGE WAS A JOURNEY, ONE THAT STARTED way before I was approached by the wonderful people at Harper-Collins who made this happen (thank you, Kate and Brad!). I have been blessed to have clients and friends—and clients who turned into friends—who kept asking, "When are you going to write a book?" before I had a chance to work it out myself. Some of those same friends have been there, along with my family, for the phone calls, draft reads, venting sessions and mini-breakdowns that it takes to get through the process of writing. There are too many of you to name, but thank you for not ignoring my calls or "leaving me on read." I hope I've expressed my thanks to you in person because I am so grateful to have you in my corner.

During the writing process, I was fortunate to be embraced by a number of mentors (thanks, Write and Ranters) who provided so much guidance and even led me to yet another editor, Catherine Oliver, who helped me declutter my brain and get this manuscript to a place where it wouldn't torture me with regret but rather make me proud.

I am so inspired by my MBA students who wrote hundreds of essays and emails affirming that our time together was fruitful and contributed to this book in so many wonderful ways, including the excerpts included with their permission.

I wouldn't have made it over the finish line without the unwavering support of my fans and followers at live events and on social media who provided encouragement and shared their success stories. They fueled my desire to empower more people and finally get this book finished. Thank you for being vulnerable with me, for trusting me, for sharing your stories with me and for your enthusiasm for the launch of this baby. I hope you'll continue to join me on this empowerment journey.

Finally, a special mention to the not-so-helpful people that have crossed my path: thank you for giving me so much practice and material for this book. I am forever grateful to you.

NOTES

1. Linda Babcock and Sara Laschever, *Women Don't Ask: The High Cost of Avoiding Negotiation—and Positive Strategies for Change* (New York: Bantam, 2007). The study was conducted by Linda Babcock at Carnegie Mellon University in 2003.

2. "Flexity Outlook (Toronto Streetcar)," Wikipedia, last modified June 22, 2020, https://en.wikipedia.org/wiki/Flexity_Outlook_(Toronto_streetcar); Ben Spurr, "Poor planning at the start bedevilled Bombardier's delivery of streetcars, TTC meeting hears," *Toronto Star*, October 24, 2019, https://www.thestar.com/news/gta/2019/10/24/poor-planning-at-the-start-bedevilled-bombardiers -delivery-of-streetcars-ttc-meeting-hears.html; Chris Fox, "Bombardier to deliver last streetcar next week, missing final deadline by just a few days," CTV News Toronto, December 31, 2019, https://www.thestar.com/news/gta/2019/10/24/poor-planning-at-the-start-bedevilled-bombardiers-delivery -of-streetcars-ttc-meeting-hears.html.

3. A note on store brands: some products are easily swapped out with the generic or store-brand version (such as Walmart's Great Value or Costco's Kirkland), while in some cases, substitution is sacrilege. If you are sharing a carton of milk with your roomie and replace it with a different brand after taking the last swig, you're fine. But you *don't* want to be the roommate who eats the last of her pal's Oreos and thinks a bag of the store-brand version is a suitable replacement. Not cool, roomie. Not. Cool. (I'm not sure if you can tell, but I have a fondness for Oreos. Who doesn't?!)

4. Robert B. Cialdini, *Influence: The Psychology of Persuasion*, rev. ed. (New York: Collins Business Essentials, 2007).

5. Adam Galinsky and Maurice Schweitzer, *Friend and Foe: When to Cooperate, When to Compete, and How to Succeed at Both* (New York: Crown Business, 2015).

6. This analogy was inspired by a diagram on page 80 of Roy J. Lewicki, David M. Saunders and John W. Minton's *Essentials of Negotiation*, 2nd ed. (Boston: McGraw-Hill, 2001).

7. Two examples are Andrea Kupfer Schneider, "Aspirations in Negotiation," special issue, *Marquette Law Review* 84, no. 4 (2004): 675–80, https://www.researchgate.net/publication/228213945_Aspirations_in_Negotiation, and Lei Lai, Hannah Riley Bowles and Linda Babcock, "Social Costs of Setting High Aspirations in Competitive Negotiation," *Negotiation and Conflict Management Research* 6, no. 1 (February 2013): 1–12, https://projects.iq.harvard.edu/files/hbowles/files/competitive_negotiation.pdf.

8. The why/motivation, how/process and what/proposal concept is inspired by the Golden Circle framework introduced in Simon Sinek's TED Talk "How Great Leaders Inspire Action," and his subsequent book *Start with Why*.

9. If you're still curious about vocal fry, you can check out an article by Arika Okrent called "What Is Vocal Fry?" on *Mental Floss* (https://www.mentalfloss.com/article/61552/what-vocal-fry). It includes a funny video with some examples. Or a *TIME* article by Markham Heid called, "You Asked: What Is Vocal Fry?" (https://time.com/5006345/what-is-vocal-fry/).

10. Criticism of Dr. Amy Cuddy's research was highly publicized shortly after her TED Talk and the end result is that the research and conclusions around how people feel and perform following power posing or postural feedback is consistent with the original findings. You can read more about it here: www.forbes.com/sites/kimelsesser/2018/04/03/power-posing-is-back-amy-cuddy-successfully-refutes-criticism and www.psychologicalscience.org/news/the-debate-on-power-posing-continues-heres-where-we-stand.html

11. Based on data reported in Nancy J. Adler and Allison Gunderson, *International Dimensions of Organizational Behavior,* 5th ed. (Mason, OH: Thomson/South-Western, 2008), 165–81.